GOOD FOOD

GOOD FOOD

MONTH BY MONTH RECIPES

By
Ambrose Heath

decorated by
Edward Bawden

London

FABER & FABER LTD.
24 Russell Square

First published in 1932
by Faber & Faber Limited
Bloomsbury House
74–77 Great Russell Street
London WC1B 3DA
This edition first published in 2015

Printed and bound by CPI Group (UK) Ltd, Croydon CRO 4YY

A CIP record for this book
is available from the British Library

ISBN 978–0–571–32392–0

2 4 6 8 10 9 7 5 3 1

TO MY WIFE
FOR HER GUIDANCE

'On ne mange bien que chez soi."

—French saying.

"Man ist was er isst."

—Old German saying.

"The ideal cuisine should display an individual character; it should offer a menu judiciously chosen from the kitchen-workshops of the most diverse lands and peoples—a menu reflecting the master's alert and fastidious taste. . . ."

NORMAN DOUGLAS—*South Wind.*

"Celui qui reçoit ses amis et ne donne aucun soin personnel au repas qui leur est préparé, n'est pas digne d'avoir des amis."

BRILLAT-SAVARIN—*La Physiologie du Goût.*

ACKNOWLEDGEMENT

A large part of this book has appeared in the columns of *The Manchester Guardian*, *The Morning Post* and *The News-Chronicle*, and the author is indebted to the Editors of those newspapers for their permission to reprint the necessary extracts.

CONTENTS

INTRODUCTION

In this little book I have attempted two things. First, to show how easy good cooking can be; and second, to demonstrate that it need not be expensive, as so many seem to think it must be. As a matter of fact, it is often cheaper in the long run, for many of the famous dishes are derived from peasant and *bourgeois* kitchens, where it was essential that everything should do its full duty, and a little always went a long way. But when I say that it may be cheaper, I am thinking not so much of single dishes, as of a series of meals which have been planned to make the most of the food which is being dealt with.

There are two essentials, however: the giving of a little time and a little trouble. Food that is

Good food, with its simplicity and perhaps unexpected cheapness, hall-marks the home of the discriminating housewife

13

INTRODUCTION

worth eating cannot usually be flung together and dished up in a hurry, and I have assumed that those who will like and use this book will be those who are ready to give some thought and care to the preparation of their meals.

It is a book for the discerning amateur, and is written to give some slight idea of the way to bring Good Food into the home. It is not intended in any way to be comprehensive, but I have endeavoured to include in it a fairly wide selection of interesting dishes which are easy to prepare and exciting to eat. There is nothing in it which cannot be cooked on a small range or on an ordinary gas oven with four rings and a grill, as my own experience has shown. Of course, if you can sport a chafing dish, or even a small methylated-spirit stove as an auxiliary, so much the better; but it is not an absolute necessity, though for some dishes, such as fruits *flambées*, it is an advantage and the former a refinement of the table.

I feel confident that this slight collection of recipes gathered from so many diverse sources will interest and be useful to at least two sorts of people, if it comes, as I hope it will, into their hands. The first are those whom our present distress has forced to take, shall we say, a more active interest in the affairs of the kitchen. They will perhaps be surprised and delighted to find that some of their old friends are still within culinary reach.

The second are those of the new generation who are now beginning to learn something of that graciousness of eating which has been lost or, rather, submerged since 1914. After such an up-heaval as that, it takes a nation a little time to settle down again to the ordinary amenities of social life; but we are gradually doing so in spite of our diffi-

INTRODUCTION

culties, and in this case we have a generation—a new class, almost—who are learning for themselves something of the value of entertaining and of the great part which food and drink play in it. The increasing popularity of the restaurants has taught them a good deal. Their gastronomic boundaries have been widened, and dull and uninventive food holds no interest for them. They want something different. There are many ambitious young hostesses to-day, in flats, in small houses, in suburban villas, who want to know more about Good Food, for their own and their friends' pleasure, and possibly—and who will blame them?—with an eye to social advancement. A certain way of achieving a reputation for discrimination lies through their ability to provide pleasant and attractive meals. To search for these in innumerable cookery books is often beyond their means or patience. To them I hope this collection will be useful.

There is a third sort of person, too, who may welcome a book like this. That is those who for one reason or another—possibly from sentiment, perhaps out of curiosity—would like to taste again in the leisure and comfort of their own homes some of the dishes which they remember having eaten with delight in a restaurant, on a holiday abroad, or in some friend's house where the food is good. Here I hope they will find a few of those dishes which so pleased them and which they can now translate to the adornment of their own tables.

The design of the book in calendar form is one of convenience only. Food which is in season is the best food of all. This should never be forgotten. Good things out of season are but a ghost of their true selves; and strawberries in cotton wool at ten shillings a pound and grouse by aeroplane at exorbitant prices are all very well for the affluent seeker after novelty (as is a new cocktail, a new cabaret turn), but no one will deny that they are a mere travesty of the real thing at the right time. So I have arranged the book in months with a table at the beginning of each, in order that the housewife may see at a glance what is in season at the moment of which she is thinking, and each month I have ventured to suggest a few seasonable dishes. Some are naturally in season all the year round, and these I have inserted in the place which has seemed to be most appropriate to them.

I ought perhaps to add that the notes in the margin under the names of the dishes do not necessarily include all the ingredients of the dish. But the major ones are there, and the notes are given to show quickly the kind of taste which one may expect—so important a factor in planning a meal or considering the idiosyncrasies of the palate.

I had almost forgotten to add a few words on the use of wine in cooking. A certain number of the recipes that follow will demand this ingredient; and to those who throw up their hands in horror at the very mention of wine in the kitchen (save for the 'trifle' consecrated by general custom to its drop of 'cooking' sherry)—to those I would say that if they cannot really afford to use a little wine in the ordinary way, then there are plenty of dishes which do not demand it, and that wonders can be worked by an ingenious cook with a little good wine vinegar. But lovers of good food will understand that it is always worth while to spread oneself a little for the sake of one's guests, and half a bottle of Chablis for one-and-nine or so will ruin no one. This modest

INTRODUCTION

outlay, combined with your own skill, will (1) give your guests enjoyment if they like their food (and being friends of yours I presume they will), (2) afford you pleasure yourself with a perfectly good excuse, and (3) increase the reputation you already have among your friends as a discerning provider of Good Food. These seem to me to be three cogent reasons for justifying this small sum: but stay! a fourth presents itself insinuatingly: you might even be able to steal a glass of it for your own luncheon! Spirits and liqueurs are rather different, but for the special dishes that need them you will be able, for a shilling or so, to buy one or two of those pretty little miniature bottles which adorn so many wine merchants' windows, or your husband could steal out to the nearest inn and buy just the quantity you needed.

I have said in my chapter on Sauces that a little adventuring does no harm. Sometimes for certain dishes there are 'short cuts' which will lead to something near the right flavour, and though I feel that I should not conscientiously recommend so unorthodox a procedure, I do believe that sometimes by these ventures comes the realisation how simple good food really is. All that is needed, as I have said, is care and a little patience. Without these virtues the most elaborate dish can be a ghastly failure; with them the most simple a surpassing delight.

A. H.

LONDON—ECCHINSWELL,
July, 1932

FOOD IN SEASON ALL THE YEAR ROUND

FISH

Sea Fish

Bream	Brill
Dory	Flounders
Halibut	Mullet
Plaice	Soles
Turbot	Whiting

Shell Fish

Crayfish	Lobsters
Mussels	Prawns
Shrimps	

MEAT

Beef	Mutton
Veal	

POULTRY

Capons	Chickens
Fowls	Pigeons

VEGETABLES

French Beans	Beetroot
Cabbages	Carrots
Cucumbers	Leeks
Lettuces	Mushrooms
Onions	Potatoes
Tomatoes	Turnips

FRUIT

Apples	Bananas
Grape Fruit	Grapes
Lemons	Oranges
Pineapples	

EMPIRE IMPORTED FRESH FRUIT

Bananas	Pineapples

JANUARY

THE FOOD OF THE MONTH

Food which is in season all the year round is given in the table on page 19.

Note.—Newcomers are printed in italics.

FISH

Sea Fish

Bloaters	Cod
Dabs	Haddock
Ling	Skate
Gurnet	Sprats
Smelts	*Whitebait*

River Fish
Eels

Shell Fish
Oysters   *Scallops*

MEAT
Pork

POULTRY

Ducks	Geese
Turkeys	

GAME

Hares	Leverets
Partridges	Pheasants
Plovers	Ptarmigan
Quails	Rabbits
Snipe	Teal
Doe Venison	Widgeon
Wild Duck	Woodcock

VEGETABLES

Jerusalem Artichokes

Broccoli	Celery
Brussels Sprouts	
Red Cabbages	
Endives	Parsnips
Salsify	Savoys

Seakale
Spanish Onions
Spinach

FRUIT

Cranberries	Medlars
Pears	*Rhubarb*

EMPIRE IMPORTED FRESH FRUIT

Apples	Apricots
Granadillas	Grape Fruit
Lychees	Nectarines
Oranges	Peaches
Pears	Plums

JANUARY

The following recipes are given during this month:

JANUARY

The calendar year opens, gastronomically speaking, in a *piano* mood, and sweeps in a gradual *crescendo* through the magnificent promise of the Spring to the *fortissimo* of early Summer, and so through the quiet *rallentando* of the gamy Autumn (a sudden *sforzando* for September oysters), when many fine flavours linger on our palate, to the almost solemn *andante sostenuto* of Christmastide and those winter days when eating is not only a pleasure, but a necessary exercise.

In January, therefore, after those permissible and gentle excesses of our modern Saturnalia, the gourmand is in a quieter and more retrospective mood, yet he is not without a sober expectation.

With January the first movement of the gastronomic symphony opens, and we look forward to the New Year's enjoyment of the table

23

JANUARY

Behind him lies the magnificence of gastronomic accomplishment; before him the prospect of new and often unexpected delights. This *piano* overture shows him facing the coming year without misgivings and without regret (unless it be a financial one), for the sure reiteration of the seasons has schooled him in the kindliest of philosophies. Nothing short of an earth-shattering catastrophe, or the diversion of the Gulf Stream, or the total eclipse of his digestive faculties can shake his absolute certainty in their unfailing return.

I repeat, without regret. If game is to be denied him (and now the last grouse has winged away, and partridge and pheasant will soon follow), well then, the birds were already past their prime, and what other and more dainty pleasures stretch out before him in a never-ending vista of culinary amplitude! Variety, after all, is the spice of *gourmandise*, and it is pleasant and comforting to think that next season's birds may be all the better for the waiting. So he will speed the parting partridge with a good heart, either *aux choux* or in the following way, which will transmogrify the oldest bird into a splendid dish.

Partridges en
Cocotte

Partridges
Sausage meat
Bacon
Onion
Carrots

Cook in a casserole for about half an hour some small pieces of bacon and sliced onions and carrots. Take them off the fire, and add a tablespoonful of good stock, some salt and pepper. Now put in the partridges, which have been previously stuffed with sausage meat, with a rasher of bacon tied over each. Cook all together with the lid on for an hour or so. When the birds are done, strain the gravy and pour it back over them in the casserole together with some button onions and lean bacon cut in small cubes, which you have meanwhile cooked in butter. Simmer the whole for a little longer, and serve in the casserole. A lovely requiem.

JANUARY

The month has its compensations for the flight of game; the return of whitebait, for instance, and of scallops. The latter will immediately be celebrated thus, by the best way of bringing out their delicious flavour. Boil them in salted water for about fifty minutes, then cut them up small and mix them with a skinned tomato, a very small onion, parsley and one or two mushrooms all chopped together. Cook this for a while in butter, season it well and bind it with a little thick Béchamel sauce. Put it back into the *coquilles*, and brown it in the oven with or without some fresh breadcrumbs sprinkled over. Nor will the grateful gourmand forget that their superior cousin, the delectable oyster (and those from the Delectable Duchy are not to be despised), is but half-way through its season.

Brer Rabbit makes a good January dish. Rather maligned, I always think he is, but he should be no more so than the guinea-fowl, whose place he seems to occupy among the quadrupeds. It must be confessed, however, that boiled rabbit, even supplemented by the cajolery of savoury forcemeat balls and pickled pork, leaves much to be desired. But he can most successfully be fried quite plainly in butter and served with more melted butter and chopped parsley, or in a more elaborate fashion, *à la Tartare*, as follows:

Cut him up and let him lie for an hour (half an hour each side) in a marinade of two tablespoonfuls of vinegar, one of olive oil, a small onion cut up, chopped parsley, bayleaf, some mace and a good squeeze of lemon juice. Take him out, dry him, egg-and-breadcrumb him, and fry him in butter. Serve, as the name denotes, with Tartare sauce.

Some may prefer a ragout *à l'américaine*. Cut the rabbit up and fry the pieces in butter till they are

Margin notes

Scallops

*Scallops
Tomato
Onion
Mushroom
Parsley
Béchamel sauce*

Rabbit à
la Tartare

*Rabbit
Vinegar
Olive oil
Onion
Parsley
Bayleaf
Mace
Lemon juice
Egg and
breadcrumbs
Tartare sauce*

Rabbit
à l'américaine

brown. Drain off the butter, pour in enough stock
barely to cover the pieces, put on the lid and cook
till tender. Meanwhile make a brown *roux* and mix
with it a cupful of tomato purée, fresh or tinned.
Take out the rabbit and keep it warm, and add to the
roux and purée about three-quarters of the stock. Stir
them together till they boil, add a pinch of sugar, a
large squeeze of lemon juice, salt, and freshly ground
black pepper. Put back the rabbit till he is hot again,
and serve in the casserole in which he has been
cooked. Rabbit Pie, Rabbit Pudding . . . his record
as a dish-maker is not a bad one. Let us catch him
while yet we may.

Rabbit
Tomatoes
Lemon juice
Stock

Seakale is the only new arrival of the vegetables,
and a distinguished one, many think. All the ways of
serving asparagus can be applied to seakale, which is
often greatly improved by a Mousseline or Hollandaise sauce. A Maltese sauce, which is made by
adding to an ordinary Hollandaise sauce the juice of
two blood oranges and a coffeespoonful of their
grated rind, is particularly to be recommended.

Seakale

Maltese Sauce

Hollandaise
sauce
Blood
oranges

Beside the usual home-grown and imported fruits,
one or two new ones come this month from South
Africa: Granadillas, whose indescribable flavour
adds a touch of real distinction to fruit salads, Nectarines, and Lychees, those odd, horny fruits with
such a charming inside.

January is the month of promise, and of new re-
solves. It would be easy—and how pleasant!—to
make a little private vow to improve our meals a
little, to give a little more trouble, a little more
thought, to their arrangement and preparation. Let
us resolve, too, to eat what is in season and so make
sure of the best. To explore the food resources of the
Empire would not be a bad resolution, either, and

we shall meet with a good many new and interesting experiences in this way. And above all let us determine to be as simple in our cooking as possible. Elaborate meals and dishes try not only the temper of the cook, but the patience and often the digestions of their consumers. By all means let the ambitious cook or hostess embark on an experiment now and then, but only within the bounds established by use. In any case, let us make up our minds to try one new dish every now and then and enlarge what might be termed our gastronomic vocabulary. And we shall find that one leads to another, till the glorious simplicity of it all dawns suddenly upon us.

To the gourmand on the threshold of the New Year this may sound trite enough. He has no pity for the martyrs to indifferent cooking. His health and jolly appetite befit him rather for proselytising than for proffering condolence. He looks serenely ahead as one meeting an old friend again, anxious to see—with what kindly interest—how the years are treating both of them. The same things, he knows, will never seem quite the same again, but from the familiarity which friendship brings with it they will have gained a richer lustre and a fresh attraction.

Pendant la nouvelle année, bon appétit, Messieurs et Dames!

*   *   *

We do not often eat fish soups in this country, possibly because we have got the idea, from tales of *Bouillabaisse*, that they are too strongly flavoured, or that they are too rich from our experience of the *Bisques* served at our more expensive restaurants.

This simple little soup is perhaps more suited to

Fish Soup

Whiting
Spinach
Onions
Carrot
Potato

Parsley
Mint
Chives

our northern palates. Chop together a handful of spinach (sorrel instead, if you can get it), one or two small onions, a carrot, a potato, parsley, mint and, if you have them, chives. Brown these in butter and add boiling water, salt and pepper. Into this put a few small whiting whole, and cook for about twenty minutes. Take out the fish, remove their skin and bones; strain the soup and serve with the pieces of fish and vegetables in it.

Garbure

Pickled pork
Haricot beans
Cabbage
Carrots
Bouquet garni

The next soup is a French regional one, and it is rightly famous. There are many ways of preparing it, but here is a fairly easy one. Cook a good handful of well-soaked haricot beans in salted water, and put in a medium-sized cabbage and a few carrots cut in small pieces. Cook on a quick fire and about an hour before you want it, put in a piece of pickled pork, some salt, pepper and a *bouquet* of parsley, thyme and bayleaf. More boiling water can be added to ensure the soup being of the right consistence. The meat and the *bouquet* must, of course, be removed before serving. I am told that peas, or turnips or potatoes can be substituted for the beans, but the cabbage and pork must be there.

Tomato Soup

Tomatoes
Onions
Water

Tomato Soup is sometimes rather a trouble to make. This version is not.

Cut a couple of large onions in slices and cook them slowly in a little pork fat for a few minutes. Add half a dozen quartered tomatoes and cook a little longer. Pour on them a pint and a half of boiling water with salt and plenty of pepper. Bring to the boil and simmer till the tomatoes are well cooked. Sieve, and serve, if you care for it, with vermicelli which has been cooked in it for five minutes. Grated cheese might well be added.

JANUARY

The hungry breakfast-eater will welcome a new thrill in the form of Eggs with Ham and Muffins.

Split and toast as many muffins as you will need. On each half place a round of fried ham, and on the top a well-drained poached or fried egg. I believe the more adventurous, greatly daring, have been known to add a Sauce Hollandaise, though this seems rather *outré*.

Eggs with Ham and Muffins

Eggs for luncheon are always nice, Eggs *à la Tripe* especially so. Cook some sliced onions (two for every three eggs) in butter till they are soft, add flour and enough milk to make a thick creamy sauce, and season it with salt, pepper and a little grated nutmeg. Into this sauce put halves, quarters or rings of hard-boiled eggs, and serve piping hot.

Eggs à la Tripe

Eggs
Onions
Milk
Seasoning
Nutmeg

Fresh Haddock can be made very delicious by using a cheese stuffing, which is made by mixing together three ounces of breadcrumbs, two ounces of grated cheese, a tablespoonful of chopped parsley, a good squeeze of lemon juice (or if preferred a dessertspoonful of tomato sauce), salt, pepper and enough beaten egg to bind them. Stuff the fish with this mixture and sew it up. Coat it with the beaten egg left over, sprinkle with browned breadcrumbs, and bake it in the oven with butter or dripping, basting it occasionally. Twenty minutes will do it, and this will give you time to make some Mustard Sauce to serve with it. A small cod can be baked in the same way, if the flesh of haddock is thought too dry.

Stuffed Baked Haddock

Fresh haddock
Breadcrumbs
Cheese
Parsley
Lemon
Egg

If you like fish with bananas, you should try Sole *Caprice*.

Have the sole filleted. Dip the fillets in melted butter seasoned with salt and pepper, and roll them in fine breadcrumbs, pressing the crumbs well on to the fil-

Sole Caprice

Sole
Breadcrumbs
Butter
Bananas

29

lets. Sprinkle with a little more melted butter, and grill them slowly till they are a golden brown. Surmount each fillet with the long half of a banana cooked in butter, and serve, if you like, with a Sauce Robert.

Mussel Pilaff

Mussels
Rice
Olive oil
Bacon
Onion
Tomato
Thyme
Bayleaf
Saffron
Parsley
Celery or
Celery salt
White wine
Cheese

Do not be afraid of Mussels in these days of rapid transport, or you will never know the joys of a pilaff of them. It needs a little trouble, but it will be well worth while.

Cook some rice, run cold water over it and let it dry. Now in a little olive oil toss three rashers of streaky bacon, which you have first blanched by boiling for a few minutes and then cut in small pieces. Put these aside and cook in the same oil a finely chopped onion, adding two peeled tomatoes cut in slices. When these are soft, season them and add a cupful of hot water, a bayleaf, a little thyme, a pinch of saffron and a lump of sugar.

While this sauce is simmering gently, put a small piece of butter in a saucepan and with it some chopped parsley, a couple of chopped shallots or onions, a small piece of celery (or some celery salt), and half a glassful of white wine. Add the mussels, scraped and cleaned, and cook for six minutes, shaking the saucepan now and then. Strain the liquor and put the mussels back into it. You can leave them in their shells or take them out, as you like. Now take a frying-pan and put all these things into it, the rice, the tomato sauce, the pieces of bacon, the mussels and their liquor, and stir well together till it is very hot, adding a little grated cheese. Serve quickly with more grated cheese sprinkled over it ... and never fear mussels again.

Beef Strogonoff

Beef *Strogonoff* has perhaps always seemed an impossibly inaccessible dish for the home, when we have eaten it at our favourite restaurant. In reality it is perfectly easy to make, as the following recipe will show. The only out-of-the-way ingredient is sour cream, which is often at hand by accident when it is least wanted! Cut some slices from a fillet of beef, beat them very flat and cut them into shortish, thin strips. Slice some onions and mushrooms and cook them slowly in butter. When the vegetables are cooked, fry the seasoned slices of beef very quickly in some butter, and add them to the vegetables with thick sour cream. If you want more 'kick' in it, a little French mustard can be included. This dish can be served with the pieces of onion and mushroom left in, but it is perhaps better if the sauce is strained.

Beef
Onions
Mushrooms
Sour cream
French mustard

Honest and oniony is the following excellent dish. Cook two large sliced onions in butter for a few minutes. Put them with half a pound of sliced potatoes in a buttered fireproof dish with a small teacupful of beef stock, salt and pepper, and cook for about forty minutes in a fair oven. Now brown on both sides some lamb or mutton cutlets, well trimmed, and bury them in the potatoes and onions. Finish the dish in the oven, cooking it till the cutlets are nicely done and the potatoes golden brown.

A little experience will tell how long this will take, and how much stock must be added in the first instance to make the dish neither sodden nor too dry, but the literally golden mean between the two.

Baked Mutton Cutlets

Cutlets
Onions
Potatoes
Butter
Beef stock

The Austrians have a pleasant dish called Goulash of Veal, which they cook in this way.

Cut about a pound of veal cutlet into dice, after removing all skin and fat, and season well with salt

Goulash of Veal

Veal
Paprika

Onion
Brown stock
Madeira or
Sherry
Caraway seeds
Bacon
Potatoes

and pepper and paprika; plenty of the latter. Fry a very small onion finely chopped in a frying-pan in butter, then add the meat and cook slowly for about a quarter of an hour. Now sprinkle on a small spoonful of flour, and pour over a small cupful of brown stock and half a wineglassful of Madeira (or Sherry would do). Add half a teaspoonful of caraway seeds in a muslin bag; or you could leave these out, if you hate the taste of them. Cover it all and leave it to cook gently. Now fry in butter a quarter of a pound of bacon cut into dice, and when it is lightly done add two or three potatoes cut into small cubes, and continue frying till they are golden. Drain them well and add them with the bacon to the contents of the frying-pan. Go on cooking till the meat and potatoes are done, stirring carefully now and then so as not to break the potatoes. Do not forget to remove the little muslin bag before serving this very delicious stew.

Chicken
Pancakes

Cooked chicken
Paprika
Mushrooms
Cream
Pancakes
Béchamel sauce
Egg
Grated cheese

If we have a little chicken over, and it is not quite enough to make a dish by itself, we should remember Chicken Pancakes.

Toss in butter some small pieces of cold chicken seasoned with salt, pepper and paprika, and, in a separate pan, some mushrooms also cut up small. Bind these together with a very little cream. Make some pancakes with unsweetened batter, stuff them with this mixture, arrange them on a dish, cover them with a Béchamel sauce enriched with the yolk of an egg, sprinkle with grated cheese and brown quickly under the grill.

Casserole of
Pigeons

Pigeons

A Casserole of Pigeons makes a good luncheon dish in cold weather.

Fry a brace of them in a casserole with a small

piece of butter and a rasher of bacon cut into little bits. Add a quarter of a pint of stock, half a pound of small quartered mushrooms tossed in butter, pepper, salt and a good glassful of claret. Cover and simmer very gently till the birds are cooked. When they are ready, strain the sauce, thicken with some brown *roux*, put back the mushrooms and pour over the pigeons.

Bacon
Stock
Mushrooms
Claret

While Chestnuts are still with us, we must try them with Brussels Sprouts. They make a good, satisfying dish.

Peel and boil some chestnuts. Boil the sprouts for a quarter of an hour, then drain them. Put an ounce of butter, pepper, salt and a little brown stock or gravy into a saucepan, and add the sprouts and chestnuts. Cook for a few minutes together, shaking but not stirring, and serve as hot as possible.

Brussels Sprouts with Chestnuts

Brussels sprouts
Chestnuts
Brown stock
or
Gravy

Potatoes are always a problem, but a little inventiveness will soon solve it. Here are three suggestions for enlivening their service.

Melt two and a half ounces of butter in a frying-pan and let it get hot enough to smoke. Then put in four cupfuls of raw potatoes chopped up fairly small. Season them and pack them into as thin a layer as possible. Put a plate over the top and cook slowly till brown and soft.

Brown Hash of Potatoes

Potatoes
Butter

Potatoes *en casserole* are unusual.

Fry in butter, in the casserole you will use, a rasher of bacon cut into tiny cubes. Chop up an onion, fry this a little with the bacon, then add two peeled tomatoes cut in small slices. Now put in some thin slices of cold boiled potatoes, plenty of salt and pepper, a piece of butter and a small tea-

Potatoes en Casserole

Cold potatoes
Bacon
Onion
Tomatoes
and possibly
Garlic

cupful of stock. Mix these ingredients well together, cover and cook for about twenty minutes in a moderate oven. A tiny piece of garlic finely chopped can be fried with the onion, if the flavour is liked.

Lyonnaise Potatoes, I

Cold potatoes
Butter
Onions

Lyonnaise Potatoes are a change from the everlasting *sautées*. *Sautez* some cooked potatoes in butter, and at the same time fry, without browning, some very thin rings of onions in another pan. When the potatoes are nearly done, add the onions to them and brown both together.

Lyonnaise Potatoes, II

Potatoes
Onions
Milk
Butter

Quite a different way of cooking potatoes *à la Lyonnaise* is as follows. Boil some potatoes in their skins, peel them while hot, slice them and put them into a saucepan. Season them with salt and pepper, and pour over them a purée of onions made by boiling some onions in milk till tender, passing them through a sieve and mixing them with butter and the liquor they have cooked in till a thin purée results. Heat this up with the potatoes, and serve.

Spinach Soufflé

Spinach
Milk
Butter
Flour
Eggs

A Spinach *Soufflé* makes a pleasant accompaniment to chicken, for instance, and is a delicious course by itself. Cook enough spinach to make two tablespoonfuls of purée. Boil a quarter of a pint of milk with two ounces of butter, and thicken it by adding two ounces of flour and a quarter of a pint of milk which have been mixed smoothly together. Boil this, add the spinach purée with the beaten yolks of two eggs and the whites of four eggs well whipped. It will require thirty minutes cooking in a *soufflé* dish.

Pilaff Rice

Among the recipes in this book Pilaff Rice will occasionally be mentioned. There are various schools of thought on this question, the to-wash or not-to-wash schools, those who introduce the

JANUARY

grains into cold water or into boiling water, and so on. They are all agreed, I believe, that the rice to be used should be Carolina and not Patna, which is more suitable as an accompaniment to curries. The principal thing to do is to see, first, that the rice revolves freely and does not catch, and second, that it is put in a sieve under the cold tap immediately it is done, so that the grains are separated. This having been done, you can, of course, add your butter, or your stock, or various flavourings according to the uses for which you intend it. It is sometimes a good tip to boil it with an onion. But you must form your own opinion on this earth-shattering problem: I will not attempt to advise. It is all a matter of temperament, and I am sure that your method is as satisfactory as mine.

But . . . here is a simple pilaff, which will be a stand-by on almost any occasion.

Having boiled the rice according to your lights, and having seen that each grain, more or less, is separate, melt some butter in a frying-pan, put in the rice with a pinch of curry powder, a good pinch of saffron, salt, pepper (black and freshly ground), a pimento cut in small pieces, a few cooked peas, a few soaked and stoned raisins, and then, O then, add whatever 'remains' you wish to sanctify by their inclusion in this noble dish: fish, lobster, prawns, or chicken, or veal, or mutton (not beef, I think). These pieces must have first been just warmed in butter, and then the whole thing is well warmed up and eaten, let us hope with gluttonous ejaculations. If you like, you can add, when you put in your pieces, a small cupful of stock and cook till it has disappeared. Personally, I think this is unnecessary.

A Pilaff of Rice

Rice
Butter
Curry powder
Saffron
Pimento
Peas
Raisins
Stock
'Remains' of fish or meat

35

Cinnamon
Apples

*Apples
Butter
Brown sugar
Cinnamon*

While we are thinking of spicy things, apples with cinnamon have an Eastern atmosphere about them.

Cut some peeled eating apples into quarters, and cook them slowly in a frying-pan in butter, turning them over now and again, till they are soft and brown. Sprinkle over them some brown sugar and a little cinnamon, and serve them after they have cooked for just a little longer.

Fritto Misto
of Fruit

We often encounter *Fritto Misto* of Meat in Italian restaurants. A *Fritto Misto* of Fruit seems to be a joyous variation. Simply take pieces of whatever fruits you like: bananas, apples, oranges, pineapples, and so on. Dip them in fritter batter and fry them in deep fat. This might be called Fritters *en surprise*, but you must be careful not to surprise your guests unpleasantly by an injudicious assortment of flavours.

Crêpes Suzette

*Pancake batter
Cream
Oranges
Curaçao
Brandy*

Chicken pancakes have, of course, reminded us of another culinary triumph, of which King Edward VII is reputed to have been so fond—*Crêpes Suzette*.

Make a pancake batter to which you have added a liqueur-glassful of curaçao. Set aside for three hours, and just before using add a little cream. Make four pancakes and keep them warm. Now melt in a chafing-dish if possible (for this last operation ought to be done at the table itself) a piece of butter, some sugar and a good squeeze of orange or tangerine juice. When this is melted, put the pancakes in one by one, turn them over once, fold them into four so that they will all lie in the dish, throw over them a liqueur-glassful of brandy and curaçao mixed, set it alight and serve these ambrosial pancakes when the flame dies down.

JANUARY

Angels on Horseback might well follow this, for few savouries bear comparison with them. Take some oysters, dust them with a little cayenne pepper, and roll each lovingly in a fragile rasher of streaky bacon. Impale one or two of these delicacies on tiny skewers, and cook them in the oven or under the grill. The piece of buttered toast which carries these angelic mouthfuls must be the horse.

Angels on Horseback

Oysters
Bacon

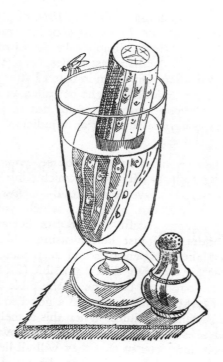

FEBRUARY

THE FOOD OF THE MONTH

Food which is in season all the year round is given in the table on page 19.

Note.—Newcomers are printed in italics.

FISH

Sea Fish

Bloaters	Cod
Dabs	Haddock
Gurnet	Skate
Ling	Sprats
Smelts	Whitebait

River Fish

Eels   *Salmon*
    Trout

Shell Fish

Oysters   Scallops

MEAT

Pork

POULTRY

Ducks	Geese
Guinea-fowl	Turkeys

GAME

Hares	Leverets
Partridges	Pheasants
Plovers	Ptarmigan
Quails	Rabbits
Snipe	Teal
Widgeon	Wild Duck
Woodcock	

VEGETABLES

Jerusalem Artichokes
Broccoli
Brussels Sprouts

Celeriac	Celery
Endive	Parsnips
Salsify	Savoys

Seakale
Spanish Onions
Spinach

FRUIT

Pears   Rhubarb

EMPIRE IMPORTED FRESH FRUIT

Apples	Apricots
Granadillas	Grapes
Grape Fruit	Lychees
Mangoes	Melons
Oranges	Nectarines
Peaches	Pears
Plums	

The following recipes are given during this month:

In the *Tableau des Gastronomes*, which someone has yet to compile, February would be one of those months which mark a definite period in the cycle of our food. For, as if in compensation for the departure of partridge and pheasant, our tables are beautified and enriched by the trout and the salmon. We have waited almost too long for this: our palates have become jaded with the perennial sole and turbot and their lesser cousins. Now the first taste, and the preliminary aroma, of a fine slice of salmon elegantly grilled makes a red-letter day for the epicure. Each year it is a sweet and virgin experience, approached only by a dish of small trout, fried gently in butter and sharpened with lemon juice and chopped parsley, *à la Meunière*. Finger-trout they

February fare brings new delights from river and sea

Trout à la Meunière

Trout
Butter
Parsley
Lemon

41

must be. A large finger, if you like; but the monsters must be reserved for boasters.

Still, we shall have to wait a few weeks before the price of these fishes is less prohibitive, and meanwhile we shall do well to remember the scallop which looks so like a bright poached egg in our fishmonger's window. A delicate shellfish is this, considered by some to have the finest flavour of all, and excellent when cooked *au gratin*, or fried, or fricasseed, or, best of all, in the Bordeaux fashion already described. We have ample consolation for our delay.

Oysters
aux Saucisses

Oysters
Sausages

Oysters are still with us, and whitebait, those pathetic little silver darlings, are coming in for frying plain or devilling. Oysters *aux saucisses* deserve to be known and acclaimed. Simply fry some good pork sausages (perhaps it is better to grill them, but this is a matter of personal preference), serve them hot, and with each bite swallow a freshly opened oyster. This Gascon predilection offers a gastronomic exercise which may well be indulged in reason, say, at luncheon.

Mussels, too, should not be despised for all their cheapness, and *soupe marinière* is a noble first course on a winter's evening. A pilaff of mussels gives something more sustaining, and the *arroz a la Valencia* of our Spanish friends is a still more ambitious (but how wonderful!) adventure in the mingling of mussels and chicken on a bridal couch of rice.

Rabbit Pie

But if our game has flown, hare and rabbit still linger with us a little. The latter simply cooked with butter and a few button onions in a casserole (so long as he is not too old) is a revelation to many to whom this ubiquitous animal is anathema. And if you are tempted to make a pie of him, try adding a few prunes stuffed with onion, parsley, fat bacon chopped together and seasoned and bound with a few breadcrumbs. Before March moves the hare to madness, he should be jugged once more. This is a dish that never satiates the eater, and we shall soon know it no more till next September.

We should perhaps allow ourselves a last piece of doe venison, for the bucks will not be ready for our tables for another five months. A good fillet larded with bacon, marinated for three or four hours in olive oil, salt and pepper and then grilled like a steak for about half an hour, is a change from the usual roast haunch and can be pleasantly accompanied by a *sauce piquante*.

Fillet of Venison

Venison
Bacon
Olive oil
Sauce piquante

For feathered fowl, if we are quick, we may get our last quails, never better than when plainly roasted under a vineleaf and a piece of fat bacon, though some prefer them stuffed with liver, truffle and chopped ham, and further enriched by a Madeira sauce. But this is painting the lily. Of the simpler birds, guinea-fowl has an insinuating flavour. It should be well larded for roasting, as the flesh is inclined to be dry. An orange salad (you will have your own ideas about this) can be eaten with it, or an Espagnole sauce. Or the bird can be boiled, and oyster or celery sauce sent in to supplement it. Wild Duck is nearly on the wing. It is sometimes a tough little creature and rather dull when roasted, but can be made extremely palatable if cooked *au porto*, that is, in much the same way as in a salmi, save that the duck is only half roasted before its introduction into the sauce.

Guinea-fowl

Veal is very good now, and there are a hundred ways of serving it. One of the simplest and most exquisite is *à la crème*, for which you take some thin

Veal à la Crème

Veal cutlet
Cream
Lemon juice

slices of fillet, well beaten, and cook them in a frying-pan in butter. When they are nicely brown, take them out and keep them hot. Scrape the pan well so as to mix the butter and the juices which have escaped from the meat, season well, and add some fresh cream. Cook a little longer and pour this over the slices. This is the best way of capturing the individual but somewhat elusive flavour of veal. Only a little potato with this, purée for choice, but a squeeze of lemon may be permitted.

**Brussels
Sprouts
à l'italienne**

Sprouts
Butter
Flour
Milk
Nutmeg
Lemon juice
Cheese

As for vegetables, Jack Frost should help our larder with Brussels Sprouts. A little grated nutmeg always improves them, and they can be varied amusingly by being cooked *à l'italienne*: that is, boiled, well drained and served in a sauce made from butter and flour, a pint of milk, seasoning, nutmeg, the juice of a lemon and grated cheese.

Fruit is not very interesting save for eating pears, which are good for cooking, baked with water and claret, or with a chocolate sauce, or *flambées* with liqueur and brandy. Rhubarb, more a vegetable than a fruit, is with us again, but a chalked notice which I saw outside a greengrocer's shop—'Rhubarb is good for the Blood'—is about all there is to say for it, except perhaps for once, very young and pink, in a pie.

*　　*　　*

Mussel Soup

Mussels
Onion
Parsley
Clove
Bayleaf

Mussel Soup is so cheap that we shall be able to afford the glass of wine we must use in it. Clean the mussels well, and cook them for a quarter of an hour or so in a pint of water to which you have added an onion, a good sprig of parsley, a clove, a bayleaf, a little thyme, salt, pepper and a glass of dry white wine. When they are cooked, take them out of their shells and keep them warm. Reduce the soup a little, strain it, and add a little cream, chopped parsley and the mussels.

Thyme
Dry white wine
Cream

Here is another simple soup, a slightly more civilised variant of a French peasant soup.

For this you want two carrots, two onions, two leeks, two tomatoes, two potatoes and a small turnip. Slice them all up and fry them for a little in butter. Now add a few sprigs of parsley, a clove, a few pounded peppercorns and, of course, salt, and gradually add enough hot water which, after boiling for about an hour, will be reduced to the quantity needed. When the soup is cooked, rub the vegetables through a sieve and either serve the soup quite plain, or enriched by a tablespoonful of cream and even still more by the addition of the yolk of an egg added at the last moment. But be sure to use water instead of stock, so as to preserve the simple flavour of the vegetables.

Peasant Soup

Carrots
Onions
Leeks
Tomatoes
Potatoes
Turnip
Parsley
Peppercorns
A clove
Water
and possibly
Egg
Cream

Here is another vegetable soup, which needs stock this time. It comes from Poland.

Fry in butter some square-shaped pieces of carrot, turnips, leeks, celery, cabbage, with a pinch of salt and sugar. Add enough brown stock to satisfy the expectant appetites, and simmer for an hour or so. Remove grease, and thicken with some browned flour mixed with a little stock. Boil up again, and after the soup has been taken off the fire, stir in a little cream.

Polish
Peasant
Soup

Cabbage
Carrot
Turnips
Leeks
Celery
or
Celery salt
Brown stock
Cream

Devilled Eggs can be prepared in two ways, at any rate. Here they are.

Cook the eggs in butter in an omelette pan, turning them over once, but seeing that they are not

Devilled
Eggs, I

Eggs
Brown butter
Vinegar

cooked too much (the yolks should be soft) and do not break. Slip them on to the serving dish, and pour over them some brown butter with a few drops of vinegar.

Devilled
Eggs, II

Hard-boiled
eggs
Butter
Cayenne
Brown gravy
Worcester
sauce
French
mustard
Parsley

The second way is to hard-boil some eggs, cut them in half lengthwise, and fill them with their own yolks mixed with butter, plenty of cayenne pepper and salt. Serve them very hot with a sauce made of thick brown gravy mixed with two tablespoonfuls of Worcester sauce and a dessertspoonful of French mustard. A little chopped parsley is a pleasant adornment.

Birds' Nests

Eggs
Bread
Butter
Cream or Milk
Parsley
and possibly
Onion

Birds' Nests are amusing for breakfast, especially if there are children about. Cut some slices of bread an inch thick and cut it out in rounds. Stamp out the centres with a smaller cutter so as to make rings. Fry these in butter till golden. Put them into a fireproof dish, break an egg into each, pour over a few drops of cream or milk, sprinkle with salt and pepper, with a little chopped parsley and (if you can face it early in the morning) some chopped onion, and bake in the oven till the eggs are set.

Cod in Cider

Cod
Olive oil
Cider
Butter
Flour
Parsley
Shallot
Mushrooms

In Brittany they have a pleasant way of cooking Cod in Cider.

Skin and bone the cod, and cut it into pieces. Put them into a casserole with a tablespoonful of olive oil and a pint of dry cider. Season with pepper and salt. Add a piece of butter about half the size of an egg which you have mixed with a little flour and parsley, shallot (or onion) and mushrooms finely chopped together. Cook all this quickly over the flame, so that the fish is done and the sauce suitably reduced at the same time.

Baked Potatoes (in the jackets) are always popular, but decidedly so when they form part of Sole Otéro.

Bake as many large potatoes as you want, cut a hole in the side of each and scoop out the contents, so as to leave the skins unbroken. Mash the potato with butter, salt and pepper. Meanwhile you have cooked some fillets of sole in the oven. These you now cut up into small pieces, mix them with some picked shrimps and moisten with Sauce Mornay. Mix this with the potato purée, refill the skins with the mixture, and heat them up again in the oven.

Sole Otéro

Baked potatoes
Butter
Sole
Shrimps
Sauce Mornay

A light dish of Oysters can be provided as follows. Heat two ounces of butter and a quarter of a gill of cream in a stewpan, and stir in a small wineglassful of Chablis, a tablespoonful of anchovy essence and some grated lemon rind. Pour half of this mixture into a fireproof dish and lay some large oysters, minus their beards, upon it. Sprinkle with grated Parmesan cheese and breadcrumbs, pour over the remainder of the sauce, add salt and pepper, more breadcrumbs and cheese, and bake briskly till browned. Serve very hot in the same dish.

Brochet of Oysters

Oysters
Butter
Cream
White wine
Anchovy essence
Lemon rind
Parmesan
Breadcrumbs

Scallops *au gratin* are a simple and digestible dish for invalids and others. Wash the scallops well and cook them gently for at least half an hour in a good white sauce. Pour it all into a buttered fireproof dish, sprinkle with breadcrumbs, or breadcrumbs and grated cheese, pour over a little melted butter and brown in the oven.

Scallops au gratin

Scallops
Béchamel sauce
Breadcrumbs
Grated cheese
Butter

A real *Wiener Fleischschnitt* is a very different matter from the lugubrious mixture of bread and meat and gravy with lank and greasy fried onions

Vienna Steak

Beef
Parsley

Mixed herbs
Nutmeg
Eggs
Butter
Onion
Flour
Brown sauce

which we know as Vienna Steak in this country. Chop very finely about two pounds of lean beef, and mix it well with a teaspoonful of chopped parsley, the same of powdered mixed herbs, a grating of nutmeg, salt, pepper, the yolk of one egg and one whole egg beaten together. Shape into flat oblong cakes, flour them and fry them in a little butter till they are cooked; then drain them and keep them warm. Meanwhile cut a large onion into rings. Coat these with flour, dip them in the beaten white of egg that you have left, again in the flour, and fry them in deep fat till lightly browned. Serve the steaks garnished with the rings and with a brown sauce. This is the best way of cooking fried onions, say for steak and onions.

Fried Onions

Brain and
Tongue
Pudding

Sheeps' brains
Sheeps' tongues
Stock or Water
Suet paste
Shallot or Onion
Parsley
Hard-boiled egg
Milk

For cold days and hungry mouths Brain and Tongue Pudding is the very thing.

Soak four sheeps' brains and four sheeps' tongues in salt and water for two or three hours, then simmer the tongues in stock or water until the skins can be taken off. Line a basin with suet paste and put in alternate layers of sliced tongue and coarsely chopped brains, seasoning each layer with finely chopped shallot, or onion, and parsley, salt and pepper. Put in here and there some slices of hard-boiled egg. Pour in a quarter of a pint of milk, cover with suet, tie up and steam for three and a half hours.

Creole Ragout
of Veal

Veal
Ham
Potatoes
Onions
Carrots

This is a very savoury Creole fashion of cooking veal.

Cut three pounds of brisket of veal into two-inch squares, half a pound of lean ham and four medium potatoes into cubes, and two large onions and two medium carrots into slices. Melt a tablespoonful of lard in a saucepan and fry the veal, seasoned with salt and pepper, till it is brown. Then add the other ingredients already prepared, with a minced clove of garlic, and let them brown together. Now mix in a tablespoonful of flour, six fresh tomatoes cut in slices, a teaspoonful of vinegar, some chopped parsley, thyme, bayleaf and marjoram, a little cayenne pepper, and a quart of water. Cover closely and let it simmer on the top of the stove for about two hours, when it will be ready for your delectation.

Lard
Garlic
Flour
Tomatoes
Vinegar
Parsley
Thyme
Bayleaf
Marjoram
Cayenne
Water

One of the famous ways of cooking sausages is with cabbage.

Sausages with Cabbage

For this you need the liquor in which you have boiled some pickled pork with a *bouquet* of parsley, thyme and bayleaf. Bring it to the boil and throw in your cabbage cut in fairly small pieces. When the cabbage is half cooked, you should have ready some grilled sausages, the kind called Parisian sausages being the best. Drain the cabbbage and chop it up with some more pepper, a little grated nutmeg and a small piece of butter. Lay half the cabbage in a fireproof dish, put in the sausages and cover them with the rest of the cabbage. Pour over a cupful of beef stock, put on the lid and cook for another half-hour in a moderate oven.

Boiled pickled-pork liquor
Cabbage
Sausages
Nutmeg
Butter
Beef stock
Bouquet garni

Another famous dish, this time Spanish, is *Arroz à la Valencia*, a mixture of fish and meat which sounds strange to us, but 'eats well', as they say.

Arroz à la Valencia (Spanish Rice)

Cook in white stock some chicken, pieces of ham, some tiny sausages and pieces of fish, all cut in small cubes. While these are cooking, chop together a large onion, some parsley and a small piece of garlic, and brown them in a deep pan in a couple of table-

White stock
Chicken
Ham
Sausages
Fish

Onion
Parsley
Garlic
Olive oil
Patna rice
Pimentoes
Tomatoes
Cloves
Mussels
or possibly
Lobster
Prawns

spoonfuls of olive oil. Add as much Patna rice as you will need and brown it lightly. Then put in two pimentoes previously fried and two peeled tomatoes, all cut into small pieces. Cook a little more, stirring now and then with a wooden spoon, and season with salt, black pepper and a little pounded cloves. Now put in the pieces of fish and meat and the little sausages cut in rounds. Add the stock they have cooked in by degrees, but do not stir any more, only shaking the pan now and again. It is finished when the rice is cooked and the stock absorbed. Cooked mussels in their shells can be used to garnish this extraordinary mixture, or pieces of lobster, or prawns, or the chicken may be in larger pieces. It should be cooked in an earthenware pan, and served in it.

Stewed
Chicken with
Chestnuts

Chicken
Water
Chestnuts

Chicken can be stewed with chestnuts to advantage.

Divide a fowl into the usual pieces and brown them in about an ounce of dripping. Pour in enough water for them to stew in, and simmer for three-quarters of an hour. Then add salt and pepper and a dozen or so chestnuts previously peeled and skinned. Cook slowly for another hour, or longer if the ingredients are not quite done. Dish up, reduce the sauce and pour it over the chicken and chestnuts.

Gibelotte of
Rabbit

Rabbit
Pork or Bacon
fat
Shallots
or Onions
Parsley
White wine

Before Rabbit goes out of season, let us eat him in a *Gibelotte*.

Joint him and fry the pieces, till they are about half cooked, in pork or bacon fat. Fry also a few chopped shallots or onions in the same fat and mix them with the pieces of rabbit, some chopped parsley, salt and pepper, and a glass of white wine, preferably Sauterne. Simmer this all for half an hour or so, when it will be ready.

FEBRUARY

This is also a good way of using up roast lamb or mutton, by simply browning the slices and substituting them for the pieces of rabbit: another revelation in the method of avoiding the ubiquitous hash.

This kind of Salmi makes Wild Duck rather more interesting.

Roast the duck, basting it well, in a quick oven for about twenty minutes. It must not be quite done. Keep it warm and make a sauce with a tablespoonful of claret and the same of port, a very little stock, a walnut of butter mixed with flour, reduced to half. Fillet the duck and *flambez* the fillets with brandy. Keep them warm while you add to the sauce any blood and gravy from the dish in which the duck was roasted and carved, a squeeze of lemon juice and a little fresh cream. Reduce slightly again, and strain carefully over the fillets.

Fried Jerusalem Artichokes offer a change from the usual garnishings for grills. Either cut them, raw, into thin slices and fry them quickly in deep fat, sprinkling the pieces with salt and pepper before serving; or fritter them in a batter made with two tablespoonfuls of flour, the same of milk, one tablespoonful of salad oil and the yolk of an egg, which has been allowed to stand for some time after being made.

This is an Italian way of cooking Leeks.

Trim and divide the leeks into pieces about two inches long, and soak them in cold water for an hour. Then cook them in boiling salted water till they are tender, take them out and leave them again in cold water for another hour at least. Drain them and dry them at the end of this time and cook them again

Gibelotte of Mutton

Mutton
Pork or Bacon fat
Shallots or Onions
Parsley
White wine

Salmi of Wild Duck

Wild duck
Claret
Port
Stock
Butter
Flour
Brandy
Lemon juice
Cream

Fried Jerusalem Artichokes

Italian Leeks

Leeks
Butter
Béchamel sauce
Parmesan
Egg

gently in two ounces of butter for ten minutes. Have some hot Béchamel sauce ready, and add to it a dessertspoonful of grated Parmesan cheese, salt, pepper, and the yolk of an egg. Mix this well together, arrange the leeks in a fireproof dish, pour the sauce over them and bake in a moderate oven till brown.

Peasant Potatoes

Potatoes
Butter or Bacon fat
Parsley
and possibly Garlic

Now for three ways of cooking potatoes.

Cut the potatoes into small pieces about an inch square, and fry them slowly in butter, or bacon fat, till they are well done and all the fat is absorbed. Just before finishing, sprinkle with some chopped parsley and, possibly, garlic.

Potato and Orange Purée

Mashed potatoes
Orange

An unusual potato purée, which is particularly good with any meat or fish dishes which require an orange accompaniment, can be made by adding the juice and grated rind of an orange to an ordinary purée. Mix it well together and serve with a little more grated rind on the top. It is pretty, and surprisingly good.

Potatoes à la Dauphinoise

Potatoes
Egg
Nutmeg
Milk
Gruyère cheese
and possibly Garlic

This is a pleasant potato dish. Put two pounds of thinly sliced raw potatoes into a basin with a beaten egg, salt, pepper, grated nutmeg, a pint and a half of boiled milk and a quarter of a pound of grated Gruyère cheese. Mix together well, pour into a well-buttered dish (which you have perhaps rubbed round with garlic), sprinkle with a little more cheese, and bake in a moderate oven for about three-quarters of an hour.

Banana Soufflé, I

Bananas
Flour

Here are two recipes for Banana *Soufflé*.

One. Cut four large bananas in half lengthwise, keeping the skins intact. Mash the flesh through a fine sieve. Now mix a level tablespoonful of flour and the same of castor sugar in a breakfast-cupful of hot milk. Bring it to the boil and cook a little longer, stirring well. When it is thick, add the yolks of two eggs, a small piece of butter, the stiffly whipped whites of three eggs, and the mashed bananas. Fill the banana skins with this mixture, and bake for about eight minutes in a hot oven. A little icing sugar can be sprinkled over each just before they are ready.

Two. Boil half a pint of milk with eight lumps of sugar. When it is cold, stir in the beaten yolks of two eggs. Mash well together the flesh of six bananas and of two sweet oranges (all pips and pith must be removed from the latter). Add this mixture to the milk and eggs, and fold in the whites of the eggs stiffly beaten. Pour into a buttered *soufflé* dish and bake in the oven in a tin of water till browned.

This unusual kind of fritter I first tasted in a little Smyrnese restaurant in London. The proprietor called them *Loucoumathes*, which I am told is a Turkish term of endearment. They certainly deserved it.

Warm half a pound of flour and a quarter of a pint of milk. Put the flour into a bowl and make a hole in the middle of it. Now mix a quarter of an ounce of yeast with half a teaspoonful of sugar, add the milk to this and pour it into the centre of the flour. Mix, and when it has 'sponged', beat in three yolks of egg and leave it for three-quarters of an hour. Knead the mixture well and let it rest for another ten minutes. It is then ready to be dropped, in tablespoonfuls, into smoking hot fat, and eaten as quickly as possible with warm honey and powdered cinnamon.

*Sugar
Milk
Eggs
and possibly
Icing sugar*

Banana
Soufflé, II

*Bananas
Milk
Sugar
Eggs
Oranges*

Loucoumathes

*Flour
Milk
Yeast
Sugar
Eggs
Honey
Cinnamon*

Orange Salad

Oranges
Sugar
Cream
Burnt almonds
and possibly
Liqueur

Let us think of something light for a change. This orange salad will do excellently.

Cut some oranges into slices, removing the pips and pith, but carefully preserving the escaping juice. Put the slices into a glass dish, and pour over them a thin syrup which you have made from the juice (with more added, if needs be) and castor sugar. Melt a quarter of a pound of lump sugar with half a tumbler of water in an enamelled pan, and boil it for about ten minutes till it is a lightish caramel. Pour it out on a dish to cool and, when it is cold and stiff, crush it rather coarsely. Sprinkle it over the fruit, cover with whipped cream, which in its turn should be adorned with splintered burnt almonds. The addition of a little liqueur, to your taste, to the oranges would be an undoubted improvement.

Cheese Pancakes, I

Batter
Cheese

Cheese Pancakes are the antithesis to the *Crêpes Suzette* of last month, but they are seldom encountered in England even on Shrove Tuesday. Two varieties have come to my notice.

The first is made simply by the addition of some grated cheese with the uncooked unsweetened batter. After you have made the pancakes in the ordinary way with this mixture, just sprinkle a little more cheese over them.

Cheese Pancakes, II

Batter
Gruyère cheese
Sugar
Eggs

The second is richer. Have ready four pancakes made with unsweetened batter. On the first spread a layer of a mixture of grated Gruyère cheese, a little salt, a little sugar and the yolks of four eggs stirred smoothly together. Then another pancake, more mixture, and so on, the last pancake being on top. This heap you cut into quarters and cook them in butter. Some add more melted butter, but as the Elephant's Child said, that would be 'too buch for be'.

MARCH

THE FOOD OF THE MONTH

Food which is in season all the year round is given in the table on page 19.

Note.—Newcomers are printed in italics.

FISH

Sea Fish

Bloaters	Cod
Dab	Gurnet
Ling	Skate
Smelts	Sprats
Whitebait	

River Fish

Eels	Salmon
Trout	

Shell Fish

Oysters	Scallops

MEAT

Lamb   Pork

POULTRY

Ducklings   Ducks
Guinea-fowls
Turkeys

GAME

Hares	*Ortolans*
Ptarmigan	Rabbits
Wild Duck	Woodcock

VEGETABLES

Jerusalem Artichokes
Broccoli
Brussels Sprouts
Celeriac   Endive
Parsnips   *Radishes*
Salsify   Savoys
Seakale
Spanish Onions
Spinach
Spring Onions
Watercress

FRUIT

Pears   Rhubarb

EMPIRE IMPORTED FRESH FRUIT

Apples	Granadillas
Grapes	Grape Fruit
Mangoes	Melons
Nectarines	Oranges
Peaches	Pears
Plums	Pomegranates

The following recipes are given during this month:

If last month it was the rivers that gave up their best
for our delight, with March begins the procession of
the fields. The country market reawakens, and lambs
and ducklings and chickens are welcome at our re-
pasts. Now the fishmonger waits expectantly for
lenten orders, and if a few minor fish have left us,
we can still contemplate with equanimity a goodly
parade headed by the noble salmon. And it is as well;
for Easter is still far away, Lent makes harsh demands upon many gourmands, and salt cod in its
pallid winding-sheet of egg sauce has too often to be
faced with as great a shudder as prompt the watery
parsnips that surround it.

Salt Cod cooked with eggs, however, is a really
admirable alternative. You make it by first boiling
your cod (after it has been well soaked, of course)

Salt Cod aux
Œufs

57

Eggs
Butter
Lemon

till it is cooked. Break the flesh into small pieces
and keep it hot. Now melt a good piece of butter in
a frying-pan, put into it six eggs beaten together
and cook slowly, stirring well as you would for
œufs brouillés. While it is solidifying, put in the
pieces of fish, some more butter, pepper, and the
juice of half a lemon. Do not keep this dish waiting:
any delay in eating is fatal to its charm.

There are one or two other attractive ways of
serving this trying fish, which appear in the following pages.

Snails

The adventurous diner-out has still a little longer
left to enjoy his favourite snails, one of the dishes
which we have inherited direct from ancient Rome.
A la Bourguignonne is perhaps a more suitable guise
from a social point of view, but the rich garlicky
taste of an *escargot* cooked in his shell is by far the
best, if one can brazenly face the outraged dismay
of one's friends and family afterwards. Frogs, too,

Frogs

can still be sought while the cold weather lasts,
strangely uninteresting little creatures, I always
think, *à la meunière*, so like a microscopic chicken in
their nearly negligible flavour, and slightly in appearance, too. But no gastronomic education can be
considered complete without them. Escoffier has a
recipe for a *chaud-froid* of them which reads very
prettily and is dignified by the name of '*Nymphes à
l'Aurore*'—fit doubtless for the rosy fingers of the
Dawn herself.

We must leave the woods alone till August, but
after our last woodcock *à la fine champagne* we can
console ourselves with the sweet simplicity of our
poussins, just spatchcocked and grilled or, more

Poussins à la
Viennoise

elaborately, *à la polonaise*, or in the Viennese fashion
cut into four, egg-and-breadcrumbed and fried, and

MARCH

served with slices of lemon and fried parsley. Next
in honour come the ducklings which, never more
delicious than when plainly roasted (with a salad of
lettuce hearts and orange or grape fruit), are de-
clared by some to reach their apotheosis when
praised with turnips and small onions. We must
wait a little longer for peas, but meanwhile we might
try stuffing our duck with an ounce of butter and a
pinch of chopped mint. A little lemon juice added
to the gravy is an improvement here. But in any
case he must be very young and cooked so that the
flesh almost melts in the mouth; and if sage and
onions must be used, then let it be, I implore you,
with discretion.

Roast
Duckling
with
Orange Salad

Roast
Duckling
with
Mint Stuffing

But the most exciting moment in March is when
we find set before us the first joint of lamb. Let
us hope it is English House lamb, but if not then
a *carré* of 'Pauillac'. . . . Ho-Ti's piglet was nothing to this most delectable experience. Having
tasted its almost unimaginable tenderness, the true
gastronome is ready to skip as innocently and as
kittishly as did the animal whose infant sacrifice
provided it.

So much for the fields. The turn of the kitchen
gardens is yet to come. Spring onions are its savoury
harbingers, and will give our salads a new sweetness
and delicacy. For those who have not tried it, an
onion tart should most certainly be attempted at the
earliest opportunity. Make an open tart of light
pastry and cook it till lightly browned. Then fill it
with the following mixture: three or four very thin
rashers of streaky bacon fried very dry and broken
in small pieces, some finely chopped spring onions
browned in the bacon fat, half a pint of milk, four
beaten eggs, salt and pepper, all mixed well to-

Onion Tart
Light pastry
Spring onions
Streaky bacon
Milk
Eggs

gether. Cook this slowly in the oven till it is firm and the top browned, and eat as quickly as possible.

Watercress is a new arrival this month, so why not watercress soup? The cress gives a charmingly fresh taste to the potatoes with which it is made. New potatoes, by the way, are as yet a mere mirage of their true selves and can only be eaten for the new adventure. Asparagus from Lauris raises a modest head, but we shall do well to bide a while.

Seakale

Seakale is very good just now, especially with mutton. An excellent way of serving it, which I recently experienced, is to accompany it when boiled with a few pickled walnuts. Among the old friends who will be leaving us soon, are broccoli,

Salsify Fritters

Salsify Unsweetened frying batter

endives, Brussels sprouts and salsify. The last should be tried as a fritter. Boil it till it is tender, and mash it well. Add to it an egg well beaten up with a tablespoonful of flour, and drop the mixture, a little at a time, into boiling fat. The result will set your friends pleasantly guessing.

March is a good month for food, but the best of it is that it is a harbinger for better ones.

* * *

Watercress Soup

Watercress Potatoes (If liked Cream Egg and Lemon juice)

This is a recipe for the Watercress Soup I have mentioned.

Cook a pound of floury potatoes till they are about three-quarters done, then add a bunch of watercress well washed and chopped. When the potatoes are done, strain them and the cress through a wire sieve and put this purée back into the saucepan with some water and cook a little longer without boiling. Cream can be added, and the yolk of an egg beaten with lemon juice. You can adorn it with a few chopped leaves of the cress and, as it is a thick-thin soup, with tiny squares of fried toast.

For the more spring-like days, a lighter soup may be preferred. For instance, a *soupe maigre*; useful for Lent, too.

Soupe Maigre

Lettuce
Spinach
Parsley
Butter
Egg

Cut two lettuces and a handful of spinach into strips and cook them with a chopped handful of parsley in some butter till they are very soft. Add hot water, salt and pepper, bring to the boil and simmer for about three-quarters of an hour. Beat the yolk of an egg (or of two) and stir into the soup when it comes to the table.

Here are two ways of cooking Eggs, the first for hearty breakfast-eaters.

For this you need morning rolls from which you have scooped out the indigestible inside. Butter them well inside and spread them with a mixture of chopped hard-boiled egg, anchovy essence and pepper, in the proportion of one egg and a dessert-spoonful of essence to each roll. Put the halves together again and bake till very hot.

Eggs in Rolls

Eggs
Breakfast rolls
Anchovy
essence

Cut some hard-boiled eggs in half lengthwise. Take out the yolk and mix it with some mushrooms (first fried lightly in butter) and tongue or ham chopped together; bind with a little cream. Stuff the eggs with this, arrange them on a bed of spinach, sprinkle with cream and some grated cheese, pour over a little melted butter and brown quickly.

Stuffed Eggs
(hot)

Hard-boiled eggs
Mushrooms
Tongue (or
Ham)
Cream
Spinach
Cheese

Now for the Fish. First, three other ways of making Salt Cod more exciting. It is assumed that the cod has first been sufficiently soaked.

Salt Cod au beurre noisette

Salt Cod
Parsley
Lemon juice
Butter

The first is simply to cut the cod into squares, roll them up and bind them with string, and boil in the usual way. Remove the string, and dish them up sprinkled with roughly chopped parsley and lemon juice and covered with lightly browned butter, or black butter, if you prefer it. Boiled potatoes with this, please.

Salt Cod à l'indienne

Salt cod
Sauce Indienne

The second is to boil a pound of the fish, and when it is cooked flake it and mix with about three-quarters of a pint of Sauce Indienne. Rice can be served with this. Sauce Indienne is made with butter and flour, a little saffron, a pinch of curry powder, milk, salt, pepper and grated nutmeg, and should have the consistency of cream.

Salt Cod à la Créole

Salt cod
Onion
Tomatoes
Parsley
Garlic
Breadcrumbs
Pimentoes
Butter
Lemon

The third is a Creole variation. Fry a minced onion in butter till golden, spread it on the bottom of an earthenware dish, and on it place three or four tomatoes which have been first fried and then finished in the oven sprinkled with chopped parsley, breadcrumbs and a suspicion of garlic, that is, *à la provençale*. Now take you flaked boiled cod, place it on the tomatoes, surmount the whole with three or four pimentoes (tinned ones will do very well), anoint with slightly browned butter and a squeeze of lemon, and heat well in the oven.

Tripe Wiggle

Tripe
Flour
Butter
Milk
Oysters

Before Oysters go out of season, there is an unusual way of serving them which deserves to be tried.

Cut a pound of cooked tripe into small pieces and add them with a good number of oysters to a white sauce made of flour, butter and half a pint of milk and tripe liquor mixed. Season this carefully and cook together for a little while. It is a noble combination.

MARCH

Salmon has been with us long enough for a slight change in his manner of presentation to be made. Two of these are as follows:

Cut the flesh into cubes of about one-inch sides, season them, and *sautez* them in butter with a few small fresh mushrooms. Half cook these pieces on the flame, then put the pan in the oven and let them finish cooking there. Drain them, and serve sprinkled with parsley and with a sauce of lightly browned butter and a little lemon juice.

Salmon à la Bretonne

Salmon
Butter
Mushrooms
Parsley
Lemon juice

Let the salmon slices lie first for half an hour or so (turn them once) in a marinade of oil and onion and parsley chopped together. When ready, anoint them with melted butter, grill one side, and before you put the other side under the gas grill, lay three or four fillets of anchovy across it.

Salmon aux Anchois

Salmon
Olive oil
Onion
Parsley
Butter
Anchovies

I have referred to Frogs and Snails, which have many enthusiastic *amateurs*. For those who wish to adventure in the land of gastronomy, or to renew an old acquaintance, these curiosities can be obtained from the Snails Restaurant, *au Bienvenu*, Greek Street, London, W. 1. The snails can be had already cooked, put back in their shells and stuffed. They only need warming up.

Frogs and Snails

This is the classical way of preparing *Caneton braisé aux Navets*.

Brown the duckling in butter and take it from the saucepan. Drain away the butter and pour in two-thirds of a pint of brown stock, the same of Espagnole sauce, a drop of white wine, and a *bouquet* of parsley, thyme and bayleaf. Put the duck back in this and braise gently for about two hours.

In the butter in which the duckling has been

Braised Duckling with Turnips

Duckling
Brown stock
Espagnole sauce
White wine
Parsley
Thyme
Bayleaf

Turnips
Button onions

browned cook a pound of baby turnips of the size of a cherry-plum (or, if they are larger, cut them to the size of a very large olive) and sprinkle them with a good pinch of powdered sugar so that they are a nice golden brown when finished. Cook also in butter twenty or so button onions.

When the duckling is half cooked (that is, after about an hour), take it out, put it into another saucepan with the turnips and onions, strain the sauce over it, and complete the cooking.

Serve garnished with these vegetables.

Poussin à la
Polonaise

Baby chicken
Forcemeat of
veal
Bacon
Liver
Onion
Parsley
Thyme
Bayleaf
Butter
Eggs
Breadcrumbs
Stock

Here is a recipe for *Petit Poussin à la Polonaise*. To cook these tender youngsters in this fashion exalts them to a high place in the gastronomic hierarchy.

Stuff each of the birds with a forcemeat made of veal, bacon, liver, a little onion, parsley, a hint of thyme and the ghost of bayleaf incorporated with breadcrumbs soaked in a little stock and some butter. Fry them briskly in butter to brown them slightly and finish cooking them in a *cocotte*.

For serving, cut them in half and keep them hot, having sprinkled them with the hot yolks of two hard-boiled eggs chopped up with some parsley. Meanwhile melt in a frying-pan a couple of ounces of butter. When this is foaming, throw in a tablespoonful of fresh breadcrumbs, fry for a second or two and pour over the *poussins*.

Woodcock
à la fine
champagne

Woodcock
Brandy
Game fumet
Lemon juice

The Woodcock *à la fine champagne* is an almost inexcusable luxury, but that should not discourage us once in a while.

Having roasted the undrawn woodcock (a little underdone), cut it into six pieces—the wings, the legs and the two halves of the breast—which you will keep hot.

Now finely chop up the intestines and press the carcase on to a pan so as to squeeze out any blood. Remove the carcase and *flambez* the rest with a glass of brandy. Reduce a little, add a tablespoonful of game *fumet*, or stock, a squeeze of lemon juice and a little cayenne pepper. Pour this mixture over the pieces of the bird and serve them surmounted by the woodcock's head.

You can serve the pieces, if you like, on toast on which the cock has been roasted, or enrich the dish still further by thickening the sauce with a little purée of *foie gras* and an ounce of butter (*à la Riche*).

Woodcock
à la Riche

(*As above with foie gras*)

If we have any cold chicken over, do not let us forget one of the simplest ways of adorning it.

Cut the chicken into small pieces. Put them in a buttered fireproof dish in which you have first built a wall of mashed potato. Cover them with Béchamel sauce, sprinkle with grated cheese and brown in the oven.

Chicken au
Gratin

*Cooked chicken
Mashed potato*
Béchamel sauce
Cheese

For disposing of cold beef, try this way.

Chop up some onions—fairly finely—fry them in butter, but do not let them brown. Add the beef cut in thinnish slices, and cook again for a few minutes. Arrange the meat on the chopped onion in the dish in which you will serve it, pour over a tablespoonful of stock, a little tomato sauce (or purée will do, if you are in a hurry). Add chopped parsley, salt and pepper. Now sprinkle fairly liberally with breadcrumbs, dot with butter, and brown well in the oven. You can wall this in with potato, too, if you like.

Beef Gratiné

*Cold Beef
Onions
Tomatoes
Parsley
Breadcrumbs
Stock*

Mutton can be treated advantageously in the same way.

Mutton
Gratiné

Pork Chops à la Maréchale

Pork chops
Butter
Parsley
Orange sauce

Grilled pork chops *à la Maréchale* must not be missed before pork 'goes out'.

Grill the chops, and just before bringing them to the table, make a few small gashes on one side and spread a mixture of butter, chopped parsley, pepper and salt. Serve an orange sauce separately.

Veal Cutlets à la Maréchale

Veal
Egg
Breadcrumbs
Parmesan cheese
Butter
Spinach
Orange sauce

Orange sauce also plays a part in Veal Cutlets *à la Maréchale*.

Brush the veal cutlets with the yolk of an egg and roll them in a mixture of half fine breadcrumbs half Parmesan cheese. Fry them a golden brown and serve with a purée of spinach, and with an orange sauce poured over the cutlets.

Braised Veal with Carrots

Veal
Carrots
Onions
Bacon
Parsley

Braised veal is more interesting than roast.

Your piece of veal, weighing about three pounds, should first be browned on all sides in butter. To this butter, when the veal has been temporarily removed, add half a dozen carrots cut in slices, the same number of button onions, a little parsley, a rasher of bacon—not too thin—cut in small bits and, of course, salt and pepper. Put in a tablespoonful of water and the veal, and cook in the oven with the lid on for just over three hours, shaking the dish now and then. Serve with potato croquettes, in the mixture of which you have added a little cheese.

Potatoes are sometimes a problem when we are all wishing it was time for new ones. The following is an excellent and simple way of cooking them, for an accompaniment, say, to a grilled *poussin*, or a hundred and one other dishes.

Potatoes Anna

Potatoes
Butter

See that the potatoes are cut into evenly thin rounds, raw, of course. Let them lie in water for ten minutes or so, then dry them and as they are dried arrange them in layers in the buttered dish in which they are to be cooked. Between each layer of potato put some little pieces of butter (do not begrudge this), and pack the layers tightly. Fill the dish to the top, over which spread some more butter. Now make the lid of the dish airtight with a paste of flour and water, and bake in a slow oven for fifty minutes. Take out the dish and, after cutting the cake in four and turning it upside down, put on the lid and cook again for another ten minutes. Serve with the melted butter poured over.

The Hungarian method of cooking potatoes is a good one, too.

Fry four ounces of chopped onion in butter, adding a coffeespoonful of paprika. Add two peeled tomatoes, sliced, and two pounds of rather thickly sliced potatoes. Just cover with stock and cook in the oven till the stock has practically disappeared. At the last minute sprinkle with chopped parsley.

Hungarian Potatoes

Potatoes
Onion
Tomatoes
Butter
Paprika
Stock
Parsley

March is not a good month for fruit, but South Africa sends us pears and peaches which, if they are not really first-class dessert fruit, are very good to 'flamber'. Thus they make an imposing-looking dish, which is really very easy to produce for the excitement and appreciation of your less-sophisticated friends.

Poires Flambées

Pears
Sugar
Vanilla pod
Liqueurs

See that the pears are unbruised, peel them, and prick them all over with a needle. Stand them in just enough water to cover them, to which you have added some sugar and a vanilla pod. Bring to the boil and cook about half an hour in a moderate oven. They should be quite soft and white, but whole. Serve them on a hot metal or glass dish, and when they come to the table pour over them a small glassful of liqueur which has been slightly warmed and set it alight. Maraschino and brandy (half and half) is perhaps the best mixture, but experiments can advantageously be made with others.

Apple Tart

Apples
Pastry
Lemon
Mixed spice
Egg
Milk
Almonds

An Apple Tart cooked in the German fashion is a pleasant change for luncheon.

To an ounce of melted butter, add the juice of half a lemon, two tablespoonfuls of castor sugar, half a teaspoonful of mixed spice and an egg beaten up with a cupful of milk. Mix this well together and put in a pound of apples thinly sliced. Let it stand for two hours. Line a round sandwich tin with the kind of pastry you use for *flans*, and fill it with the mixture. A few blanched almonds should be dotted over the top, and the whole thing baked in a fairly hot oven for twenty minutes or so. The almonds and the spices give the tart a delicious and unexpected flavour. Cream should be served with it, and it is better eaten hot.

Zambaglione

Eggs
Madeira or
Marsala
Sugar
Lemon

Here is a sweet, of which many of us read for the first time in a conciliatory scene in *The Constant Nymph*, a pleasant after-the-theatre concoction, Zambaglione, cousin to the French *Sabayon*.

For eight people take six eggs, two glasses of Madeira or Marsala, nine ounces of castor sugar and the juice of a lemon. Whip the whites and put them with the rest of the ingredients into a thick saucepan. Cook this over a very slow heat—a methylated spirit stove is best—beating and stirring all the time. Do not let it boil, and do not stop stirring till it is really thick, when you and your adoring guests must eat it hot out of warmed glasses.

Fondue

Brillat-Savarin in his *Physiologie du Goût* tells of an

68

amusing episode with a '*Fondue*', after which he gives the following recipe for this famous dish:

Gruyère cheese
Eggs
Butter

Take as many eggs as the number of guests demands, weigh them in their shells, and have ready some grated Gruyère cheese a third of the weight of the eggs and a piece of butter a sixth of their weight. Break the eggs into a casserole and beat them well together; then add the cheese and the butter. Put the casserole on a spirit stove and stir continuously till the mixture is thickened: add a little salt and a good deal of pepper, 'which', he says, 'is one of the definite characteristics of this ancient dish'. Serve on a lightly heated plate.

It is a convivial dish, for the author adds, '*faites apporter le meilleur vin, qu'on boira rondement, et on verra merveilles*'. Custom has it that this dish should be eaten with a fork, but in some parts of Switzerland the guests are supplied with small pieces of dry toast which are dipped in the common dish of fondue. If by mischance a piece of toast is dropped into the fondue, the careless guest must pay for drinks all round.

* * *

A NOTE ON COOKING ON SKEWERS

The primitive has a fascination for us all, but it is usually in its more unpleasant manifestations that we encounter it nowadays, and cooking is the last form in which we should be prepared to welcome it. But now and then we meet it in scant disguise among the elaborations of our civilised age, and its very simplicity gives it a greater attraction.

COOKING ON SKEWERS

Cooking on skewers is a case in point. We have travelled far from the day when the hungry hunter thrust his flesh-laden spear into the blaze or the mercenary's sword roasted his hard-earned ration before the camp fire. These barbarities may, we think, ill suit us, save in cinema-Russian banqueting scenes or in our ultra-modern grill-rooms where a pseudo-Cossack parades our skewered meat in majestic and cartridge-corseted array.

Yet this primitive form of cooking is still among the easiest and most savoury, though too few of us attempt it in our homes. Angels on horseback—those snugly blanketed darlings—are perhaps the nearest we get to it, they and their cousins the devils, though the oyster rides more cosily in its fragile bacon rasher than the stuffed prune, I always think.

Skewered meat as we know it derives from the East, where it is still commonly served under the name of Kebab. The first appearance of the skewerful of morsels only prepares us for the genuine thrill, quite primordial, when the meat is slipped off on to the steaming pilaff of rice without which it should never be served. And the thrill can be there without any glamorous surroundings. No Eastern banquet, no fashionable restaurant is needed. Our own table is a fitting altar for this literally burnt sacrifice.

All that is needed are a few skewers of silver or stainless steel or thin wood, and a grill. You need not even have a grill, for the laden skewers can be suspended in the oven, though the flavour is not quite the same. Let us take meat first. The real near-Eastern Kebab consists usually of pieces of lean mutton, in cubes of about an inch or an inch and a half, shavings of raw onion, and slices of tomato, speared alternately on each skewer till it is full or the capacity of each eater properly estimated. Pepper-and-salt it and sprinkle with the tiniest pinch of thyme. Grill it on all sides, first putting it into the flame to ensure that delicious burnt taste, and serve on a pilaff of rice, allowing a skewerful to each diner. Bring it to the table on the skewers, from which the meat is slipped on to the rice.

This is the easiest way, but you can vary it. For instance you can use, in this order, pieces of bacon rashers, apple, mutton, and onion, having first sprinkled them with curry powder, ground ginger, and salt, and left them for a couple of hours. Or you can skewer your mutton between pieces of streaky bacon and bayleaves. Or, forsaking mutton, you can use veal, or liver, or kidneys. The veal you skewer between pieces of bacon, or alternately veal, bacon, and liver—the 'brochettes Parisiennes' of student days in the Gay City. Or plain liver separated by bacon, this with fried potatoes, say, for breakfast. Chickens' livers can be treated in the same way. Or for the liver substitute kidney (sheep's kidney, or veal kidney, which many consider more delicate). What a good start for the day!

Nor need we confine our skewer experiments to meat. For the fish course we might try alternating pieces of lobster with thin slices of mushroom (and if you like and can afford it, slices of truffle), egg-and-breadcrumb them and fry them. For the savoury course there are any of the following. Angels on horseback, devils on horseback, or in the bacon wrapping can be introduced chickens' livers or chopped ham or mushrooms or potted meat mixed with breadcrumbs and bound with the yolk of an egg. These can be made more attractive by pinning

71

each one with a single tiny skewer instead of serving them all on a long one.

The ingenious will be able to amplify this list of unusual dishes after a few experiments. In spite of the increasing intelligent interest in food and the manners of presenting it, we are still prone to fall back on the usual uninventive dishes, not so much because we like them, but because we do not realise how simple it is to vary them. Here is a chance of delighting your friends with some quite novel dishes. Besides, they are excellent.

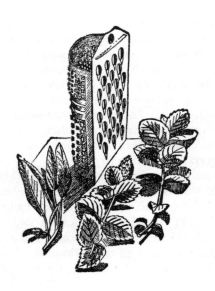

APRIL

THE FOOD OF THE MONTH

Food which is in season all the year round is given in the table on page 19.

Note.—Newcomers are printed in italics.

FISH

Bloaters	Dabs
Hake	Ling
Mackerel	Skate
Smelts	Whitebait

River Fish

Eels	Salmon
Trout	

Shell Fish

Crabs	Oysters
Scallops	

MEAT

Lamb	Pork

POULTRY

Ducklings	Guinea-fowl

GAME

Ortolans	Ptarmigan

VEGETABLES

Jerusalem Artichokes	
Asparagus	Horseradish
Parsnips	Radishes
Seakale	
Spanish Onions	
Spinach	
Spring Onions	
Watercress	

FRUIT

Rhubarb

EMPIRE IMPORTED FRESH FRUIT

Apples	
Avocado Pears	
Granadillas	Grapes
Grape Fruit	Limes
Melons	Oranges
Peaches	Pears
Persimmons	Plums
Pomegranates	
Quinces	

The following recipes are given during this month:

We are still on the threshold of Spring. The jolly lambkin, whose younger brothers leapt so artlessly to our table in March, now gambols a hint more sedately, but his flesh is nearly as delicious. Grass will give him a new flavour, and nowhere in the world is better grass lamb to be found than in England. The first spring sunlight slants on the homing drifters, their holds shimmering with the rainbow mackerel, a newcomer to our fishy fare. Happy days when we sauntered home from the quay with ten mackerel skewered through the gills on ten fingers, and happy the faintly oily taste of him fresh from the seal Grilled he is at his best, with *maître d'hôtel* butter; but the Germans have a way of stuffing him with breadcrumbs, minced onion, parsley, lemon juice, salt and pepper, and cooking him *en papillote*, serv-

Stuffed
Mackerel

*Mackerel
Onions
Breadcrumbs
Parsley
Lemon
Bread sauce*

75

Mackerel
au Whisky

Mackerel
Parsley
Shallots
Butter
Whisky

ing him out of his paper wrapper with bread sauce. Odd, but very palatable. I do not think I will try him grilled, covered with chopped parsley and shallots, a good piece of butter, a spoonful of water, salt, pepper and a liqueur-glassful of whisky and the sauce reduced in the oven, as M. Alin Laubreaux has suggested; but the adventurous may like to do so.

Of other fish there is little new. The noble sturgeon makes horny appearance, but scarcely ever in this country save as a curious adornment of some enterprising fishmonger's window. Hake, another fresh arrival, is to my mind a better substitute for cod in certain made-up dishes. Eels and sprats have left us, and oysters alas! are going soon. Let us collect the last few doleful dozens against the summer

Hot Crab

Crab
Mustard
Shallot
Parsley
Breadcrumbs
Butter
Cayenne pepper
Cream

months. Crab, however, comes in, and very good he is, though excluded from any of the classic dishes. Perhaps best plainly dressed, he can be eaten hot in the Creole fashion, or in the following simple manner. Chop the flesh as finely as possible and mix it in a bowl with a little plain mustard, in the proportion of a small teaspoonful to a large crab. Now mince a shallot and a little parsley and add it to the mixture with half as much fine breadcrumbs as there is crab. Meanwhile you should have melted about three ounces of butter. Pour this into the mixture of crab and breadcrumbs, stirring well till the *liaison* is complete, pepper it well (a little cayenne for those who like it hot in every sense of the word), and at the last add a little thick cream. Put this mixture back into the crab shells, or into separate *coquilles*, sprinkle with breadcrumbs, pour over a little melted butter, and cook in the oven—about five minutes— to brown. Admirable! Try it!

APRIL

Lobsters, too, will help to console us for the oyster's loss: hot in so many entrancing disguises, *à l'américaine, à la broche, à la Russe, Newburg, Mornay, au gratin*—till the warm weather inters him fragrantly in aspic and embalms him in salads and *mousses*.

But to return to our lamb. Even the tenderest and most succulent roasts must pall at last, though they be varied *aux pointes d'asperges*, that is, the lamb baked in a casserole on a bed of sliced carrots, onions and bacon, and served with a covering sauce composed of the gravy, a thick Béchamel and asparagus tips *sautées* in butter. Another variation may be achieved by spreading over the roast lamb a mixture of breadcrumbs, minced parsley and garlic and by cooking it for another quarter of an hour till this pleasant covering is golden.

Pork will soon be out of season, so this month we should not forget a few farewell dishes; some fried egged-and-breadcrumbed pork cutlets on a bed of onion purée, or grilled ones with orange sauce, *à la Maréchale*. The weather may even permit a noble Crown Roast to glorify his departure, a *pièce de résistance* which none can resist. For a lighter dish, more in the nature of a brief but tearful goodbye, the Danish *Frikadeller* might be tried; little fried egg-shaped cakes of minced pork mixed with egg, flour and milk, dished up on a purée of spinach or potato, and served with tomato sauce and pickled peaches.

As for vegetables, those of summer are still enshrouded, but very young carrots and turnips can be carefully considered. The gourmand is the gardener's enemy, for his instinct is to despoil everything long before it reaches maturity and exhibition

Roast Lamb
and
Asparagus
Lamb
Carrots
Onions
Bacon
Béchamel sauce
Asparagus tips

Roast Lamb
Persillé
Lamb
Breadcrumbs
Parsley
Garlic

Pork Cutlets
with
Onion Purée

standard. Never mind! Carrots are, I believe, good for the complexion and the figure, so they should be in the fashion nowadays unless by the time this appears we are returning to Victorian contours. They are not very exciting to my mind, a flavour which is neither one thing nor the other, sweetish, feminine, mawkish. Turnips, on the other hand, have an entirely masculine flavour, peppery and very definite, delicious not merely as a vegetable course, their harshness softened with butter, but as a soup, simple enough, which will shame most others at this time of year. Cook in butter, but not long enough to brown them, six young turnips quartered. Add plenty of salt, a nice piece of butter and a pinch of sugar. Fill up with boiling water and simmer for four hours. When it is done, pass the turnips through a fine sieve and water them down with the liquid they have cooked in till the soup has the right consistency. Tiny cubes of fried toast with this, please, and you can enrich it if you like with an egg yolk beaten with a little cream.

Young Turnip Soup

*   *   *

Our young Turnip Soup has reminded us of his relation, the carrot. This is a Carrot Soup very suitable for April weather, if you like the flavour.

Scrape a pound of small carrots and put them into two and a half pints of water with two onions, a bayleaf, salt and pepper. Boil up and simmer for three or four hours. Sieve the carrots into another saucepan and strain the soup over them. Cook for a little longer, and serve, adding the yolk of an egg if you like.

Young Carrot Soup

Carrots
Onions
Bayleaf
Water
and possibly
Egg

APRIL

Cheese Soup in France is simply *consommé* into which the vegetables and spaghetti, macaroni or vermicelli have been added and cheese grated over, a kind of emasculated *Minestrone*.

Cheese Soup,
I

Consommé
Vegetables
Vermicelli
Cheese

There is another kind of cheese soup which is worth trying. Fry a small finely chopped onion in an ounce of butter without browning it, then add a pint of milk and a pint of water. When this is nearly boiling, stir in two slightly beaten eggs, two ounces of grated cheese, and some salt and pepper. After adding the eggs and cheese you must not, of course, boil the soup, which on serving may be fortified by slices of French roll well dried in the oven.

Cheese Soup,
II

Onion
Milk
Water
Eggs
Cheese
French roll

Eggs *sur le plat* with cheese and onions make a good dish for luncheon. They are usually served in small shallow individual dishes, or on a dish which will conveniently hold three or four eggs. On to one of these latter sprinkle a good tablespoonful of minced onion which has been cooked, but not browned, in butter. Break the eggs over this, sprinkle them with a little grated Parmesan cheese, and cook quickly in the oven until the eggs are set and the cheese slightly browned.

Eggs with
Cheese and
Onions

Onions
Eggs
Cheese

For a more substantial dish you will prefer this Spanish omelette, especially when spring onions, its crowning touch, are very young.

Fry in butter half a pound of thinly sliced new potatoes. When they are ready, add a quarter of a pound of finely chopped cooked ham. Season with cayenne pepper, or paprika, and a very little salt. Beat four eggs lightly, pour them over the potatoes and ham, and cook in the frying-pan till they are just set. Insert a slice under the omelette and turn

Spanish
Omelette

New potatoes
Cooked ham
Cayenne or
Paprika
Eggs
Spring onion

the whole thing over on to a hot dish. Finally, and most important, sprinkle it with the finely chopped green part of a very young spring onion.

Trout à la Meunière with Bananas or Mushrooms

Trout
Butter
Lemon
Parsley
Bananas or
Mushrooms

Although many will swear that there is nothing to beat Trout cooked *à la meunière* (and it is very hard to confute them), some will permit the addition of banana to this exquisite dish. Cook the trout as you would for *à la meunière*; that is, dip them in milk, roll them lightly in flour, season them and fry them in butter. Pour over the trout the butter in which they have cooked, flavoured with a good squeeze of lemon juice and some chopped parsley, and lay on each fish the long half of a small banana which you have meanwhile cooked in butter. Slices of button mushrooms tossed in butter can also be used as a garnish in place of the bananas.

Brandade of Salt Cod

Salt cod
Oil
Garlic
Milk

There is one famous dish of Salt Cod which I forgot to give last month. It is called *Brandade de Morue*, and although the salt cod we get in this country is not quite the same as the *morue* to which the title refers, we shall not go very far wrong in using it.

Flake a pound of cooked salt cod and keep the pieces hot. Have a saucepan ready with the sixth of a pint of oil and, when the oil is smoking, add the cod and a piece of crushed garlic the size of a pea and stir over the fire with a wooden spoon till the fish is well shredded. Keep on stirring and take the saucepan off the fire and, still stirring, add to the mixture, as you would for mayonnaise, about half a pint of oil, drop by drop. When the mixture gets too stiff, add now and then a tablespoonful of boiling milk. When the *brandade* is ready, it should be as thick as potato purée. See that it is well seasoned, and serve with *croûtons* of fried bread. This is a strong hint for Good Friday.

This is a Fish Custard which is handy for using up cold fish. But it is better to boil the fish especially for it, so that you can use the stock for the custard. Cook the trimmings of the fish in a pint of milk. Only half cook the fillets. Make a custard with this liquor and one egg, put the fillets into it, and bake in a tin of water for three-quarters of an hour. The custard can be improved by the addition of a little curry powder, and this in turn might be improved by boiling an onion with the fish trimmings. A *bouquet garni*, too, you will be able to suggest . . . and so on. That is how great dishes are evolved.

Fish Custard

Fillets of Fish
Fish stock
Egg
Milk
and possibly
Curry powder
and/or Onion
and/or
Bouquet garni

Something fried, for a change. Raise the fillets on one side of a small plaice without removing them, and crack the backbone at each end. Flour, egg-and-breadcrumb the fish and fry it in deep fat till golden. Now take out the backbone, and stuff the cavity between the fillets with a mixture of the yolks of two eggs, hard boiled, four boned and pounded anchovies (or some anchovy essence) and two ounces of butter.

Fried Plaice with Anchovies

Plaice
Hard-boiled eggs
Anchovies
Butter

Oysters might very well make their last appearance at our table this month in a fashion which hails from a country where they are never out of season. Simply cook some mushrooms in butter and poach an equal number of oysters lightly. Top each mushroom with an oyster and serve either plain on little pieces of buttered toast, or with a brown or Béchamel sauce.

Mushrooms and Oysters

Mushrooms
Oysters and possibly Brown or Béchamel sauce

Large mushrooms can also be most appetisingly useful with scallops. Stew some scallops, chop up the white and red parts and keep them separate,

Mushrooms and Scallops

Mushrooms
Scallops
Béchamel sauce
Parsley

bound very lightly with a little Béchamel sauce. Cook some large mushrooms in butter, and when they are done pile first the white, then the red part of the scallops on each of them. Serve very hot, with a final flourish to the colour scheme by a sprinkle of parsley.

Fried Scallops

Salad oil
Lemon
Parsley
Egg and
breadcrumbs

Scallops can be fried, too. Marinate them for half an hour in a mixture of salad oil and lemon juice seasoned with salt and pepper. Turn them two or three times. Drain them, roll them in flour, egg-and-breadcrumb them, and fry them golden in boiling fat. Serve with fried parsley.

Spanish Beef
Steak

Steak
Onion
Rice
Hard-boiled Egg
Gherkins
Breadcrumbs
Olive oil
Paprika

Here is a Spanish way of cooking beef steak.

Get a thick slice of steak, about a pound, and beat it out flat. Now spread on it a mixture of chopped onion, boiled rice, finely chopped hard-boiled egg, two chopped gherkins and a cupful of breadcrumbs previously soaked in olive oil. Season well, roll it up and tie it round, sprinkling the outside with flour and paprika. Melt some dripping in a baking-dish, put in the steak and bake for fifteen minutes in a hot oven, turning it over after the first five.

Fried Tripe

Tripe
Oil and vinegar
Egg and
breadcrumbs
or Batter

Tripe-despisers should try fried tripe, which I first tasted at the Carlton Hotel, in London, not in Chorlton-on-the-Wiggle. (This remark is made not out of snobbishness, but as a recommendation of fried tripe!) It is extremely good, and is certain to convert them to frenzied tripe-eating, so long as they do not know what they are eating till after it is all over. Cut some well-cooked tripe into thinnish strips, and soak them for a little in a fifty-fifty marinade of oil and vinegar. Drain them, coat them with flour, and either egg-and-breadcrumb them or dip them in batter, and fry them to your appetite's content.

Liver, another 'offal', can be deliciously baked. It must be Calf's liver, and if you cook it in this way it will never turn out leathery, as it often does when fried. It will be more savoury, too.

Baked Liver

*Calf's liver
Streaky bacon
Parsley
Onion or Shallot
Butter*

Fry the pieces of liver quickly in butter, so that each side is just browned. Chop together a rasher or two of streaky bacon, some parsley and an onion or, better, a shallot. Season and spread this mixture on the bottom of a flat fireproof dish. Place the slices of liver on this fragrant bed and anoint them with the butter in which the liver was fried. Cover with buttered greaseproof paper and bake in the oven for about a quarter of an hour. A simple, well-mashed (no lumps!) and not too buttery purée of potato is the perfect accompaniment to this exceptional dish.

If you want a fascinating way of serving chicken, here is one. It is quite easy, but needs great care.

Cassolettes of Chicken

*Potato purée
Cooked chicken
Mushrooms
Cream
Parsley*

Make some purée of potato as for *croquettes*, and roll it into medium-sized balls. Shape these into the form of small drums, egg-and-breadcrumb them and fry them in boiling fat till they are golden brown. (Do not put in too many at once, or the temperature of the fat will drop.) Now carefully remove one end of each little drum, and even more carefully scoop out the inside. Then refill them with a delicately flavoured mixture of finely chopped cooked chicken and tossed mushrooms bound with a little cream. Put the *cassolettes*, as they are called, back into the oven for a few minutes, and serve with fried parsley.

Pork and Beans

Haricot beans Pickled pork Treacle or Sugar Mustard Water

Cassoulet, however, is a very different matter. It is a kind of prolonged and elaborate stew of haricot beans, pork, goose, mutton, even partridges, hare, venison and heaven knows what, in the preparation of which many French towns and districts strive in gastronomic rivalry. There is even a *cassoulet* of Fish, too, but the one with which we are all familiar by now, though by another name, is our dear old friend, Pork and Beans. It is probably cheaper and certainly easier to depend for the supply of this on the all-providing Mr. Heinz, but if you would care to try making it yourself, I am told that if you soak the haricot beans for twelve hours and next day put them in an earthenware *cassole*, or jar, with a piece of pickled pork, salt, pepper, two spoonfuls of treacle or sugar and a spoonful of made mustard, a covering of water and very slow cooking for twenty-four hours will produce the Right Thing. (Possibly your favourite baker would cook it for you, if his oven would do—which I do not know.)

Haricot Beans

After this lengthy process, Dumas' favourite method of cooking Haricot Beans seems simpler. That was to mix a pound of pickled pork cut in slices with a quart of soaked haricot beans, and to cover them with water and cook slowly till all the water was absorbed and the beans cooked. But, after all, this may turn out to take just as long, though I doubt it.

Stuffed Potatoes with Sausagemeat

Potatoes Sausagemeat

Pork figures again in our first Potato dish this month.

Peel some fairly large old potatoes, cut them in half lengthwise and scoop out a goodly hole in each half. Stuff this hole with sausagemeat to which you have added some chopped parsley (and a little chopped garlic), and bake the potatoes with a tea-cupful of stock in a fireproof dish for about an hour, basting them pretty often. The oven should be a moderate one.

Parsley and possibly Garlic Stock

The usual Potato Cake of mashed potato cooked in a frying-pan with a plate over it is varied in Poland by the addition of a chopped hard-boiled egg and two chopped boned anchovies to each pound of potatoes. Or this mixture can be shaped into smaller cakes and fried in boiling fat.

Polish Potato Cake

Mashed potato Hard-boiled egg Anchovies

Spinach can be usefully combined with potatoes, by adding a purée of spinach with butter and cream to the usual potato purée. This might be very nice with the *cassolettes* described above.

Spinach and Potato Purée

We are familiar with baked apples and pears, but Baked Oranges are not so common on our tables. Just cut off the top of each orange, insert a little lemon juice mixed with sugar, put on the tops again and bake in a casserole with a little water and sugar. Whipped cream is suggested with this dish.

Baked Oranges

Oranges Lemon and possibly Whipped cream

A pleasant German pudding can be made with any kind of tinned fruit, or fresh fruit when it is in season. It is called *Kuchen.* You make an ordinary batter, as you would for Yorkshire Pudding, adding a little sugar and two tablespoonfuls of melted butter. Put it into a shallow fireproof dish and place over it pieces of the fruit you wish to use. Sprinkle with plenty of fine sugar and powdered cinnamon, and half a cupful of coarsely chopped walnuts. Bake in a moderate oven for three-quarters of an hour and serve with cream, custard or an appropriate sweet sauce.

Kuchen

Tinned fruit or Fresh fruit Batter Cinnamon Walnuts

Baked Pears with Chocolate Sauce

Pears
Vanilla pod
Chocolate

Baked Pears are very delicious with chocolate sauce. Either bake the pears separately and pour a chocolate sauce over them before serving, both hot, of course; or prepare them in this way, which gives a more subtle flavour.

Cook some peeled, cored and quartered pears with a very little water, sugar and a vanilla pod. When they are nearly done, take them and the vanilla pod out, and melt in another saucepan some finely grated chocolate with a spoonful of the water in which the pears have been cooking. Pour this into the first saucepan, add a little butter and the pieces of pear, and sweeten a little more if you think it needs it. Continue cooking very slowly till the pears are quite done and the sauce creamy. Serve at once.

Orange Jumbles

Almonds
Sugar
Butter
Flour
Oranges
Cochineal

A useful, and delicious biscuit which can be served with cream or fruit is the Orange Jumble. To make these shred a quarter of a pound of almonds and mix them with the same amount of white sugar, three ounces of butter, two ounces of flour and the grated rind and juice of two oranges. Mix this well together and colour with a drop or so of cochineal. Drop this mixture by teaspoonfuls on a greased baking-tin, and bake in a fairly slow oven till the biscuits are done. They should be set pretty widely apart in the tin, as each will spread out to about the size of a teacup rim. To say that they are indescribably charming really describes them.

Devilled Biscuits

Butter
Chutney
Worcester sauce
Water biscuits

The same discriminating source that supplied these adorable Jumbles also provides directions for Devilled Biscuits. Make a paste with a tablespoonful of butter, a teaspoonful of chutney and a dash of Worcester sauce. Spread this thinly on some very thin water biscuits, and put them into a hot oven for five minutes. A supply of radishes and cold cream-cheese provides the proper foil.

Bananas with cheese make a slightly heavier savoury. It is a combination which you will either like inordinately or detest. Try your luck, first, by eating a piece of cheese with your next banana. Here is the savoury.

Melt some butter, with salt and paprika, in an earthenware dish. Add a few peeled bananas halved lengthwise, sprinkle with breadcrumbs and grated Parmesan and Gruyère cheese, pour over a little melted butter, and cook in the oven till browned.

Bananas with Cheese

Butter
Paprika
Bananas
Breadcrumbs
Parmesan and Gruyère cheese

MAY

THE FOOD OF THE MONTH

Food which is in season all the year round is given in the table on page 19.

Note.—Newcomers are printed in italics.

FISH

Sea Fish

Hake	*Herrings*
Mackerel	Smelts
Whitebait	

River Fish

Eels	Salmon
Trout	

Shell Fish

Crabs	Scallops

MEAT

Lamb

POULTRY

Ducklings
Guinea-fowl

GAME

Ortolans

VEGETABLES

Jerusalem Artichokes
Asparagus *Green Corn*
Green Peas Horseradish
Parsnips *New Potatoes*
Seakale
Spanish Onions
Spinach
Spring Onions
Watercress

FRUIT

Green Gooseberries
Rhubarb

EMPIRE
IMPORTED
FRESH FRUIT

Apples
Avocado Pears
Granadillas Grapes
Grape Fruit Limes
Melons Peaches
Persimmons Pears
Pomegranates
Quinces

The following recipes are given during this month

With May, I always think, should begin the gastronomic year, the *Annus Edibilis* of the poet yet unborn.

It is a month of simple delights. Let us eschew the unusual or uncommon, such as the rich and rare lamprey, killer of a gourmand king, and rather let us sing of his less extravagant brothers, the noble salmon and the knightly trout, the gracious sole, the plainer plaice and, for the more seasonable days, the lobster, that master of delectable disguises, the less known but often more delicious *langouste*, the tender little crayfish, the succulent prawn and their coarser cousin, the crab.

Indeed, the fishmonger's month is May, though oysters, alas! are gone, and with them the less-re-

The month of May begins a new period in the gastronomic cycle, and cajolingly commands us to be merry in it

93

gretted skate, a pleasant if unsightly fish of which we should resolve to eat more when next we meet. Herrings, wrongly despised by some, now come into season: and excellent they are in many ways, fried or grilled or stuffed with forcemeat or with his own roe chopped up with buttered egg and then baked in the oven, or in a pie-dish baked with tomatoes. He is always a good plain luncheon dish, and his creamy roe makes a savoury fit for the gods. Recipes will be found elsewhere.

There is no rival in the world to English lamb and he still holds pride of place on our tables; but veal, and its sweetbread, are a happy thought for lighter dishes on sultrier days. Pork is no more, though the sausage, breadier and more vinegary, persists; but the version in the form of the rotundity of hams, York, Bradenham and the exquisite Virginian, will grace our sideboards more and more, we hope.

Game takes a holiday: even the harsh-fleshed ptarmigan has gone. (What virtue could there be in a bird with a name like that?) It is true that we can serve imported game, but it is a poor substitute. I repeat: eat what is in season, and you will eat what is best. Besides, what would become of the thrill of the first autumn birds?

Spring Chicken à la Clamart

Chicken Peas à la française

Spring Chicken au Lard

Ducklings and Spring Chickens greet us in an ecstatic chorus, eager for their funereal couch of green peas. For two Maytime delights in one, cook a spring chicken with butter in a casserole, and when it is half cooked put in some half-cooked peas *à la française*, and finish cooking all together. You will swear you have tasted nothing better. Another way for spring chicken is to cook him with bacon fat instead of butter and with some potatoes cut into

MAY

small rounds about the size of an olive; or stuff him with sausagemeat, brown in butter and finish cooking *en casserole* in the oven, with the addition towards the end of a few quartered and *sautés* mushrooms.

Spring Chicken stuffed with Sausagemeat

But May is perhaps merriest when we make sweet reacquaintanceship with the springtime vegetables, those youthful blessings of the soil. New potatoes, tenderskinned and waxy, are coming into their own at last. Asparagus lends its peculiar charm to our board, whether severely alone or the dainty sprew to flavour and adorn the other courses. If some of us are fortunate enough to tire of it, let them not forget that there are other ways of treating it than by serving simply boiled or steamed. It can, for instance, be frittered, or cooked *à la crème* or *au gratin*. Nor need they confine its accompaniment to melted butter or *sauce vinaigrette*: there are other sauces. And yet—it is almost perfect when plain; and what could be nicer and more refreshing than a silver dish of iced asparagus after the play?

Green peas it is impertinent to praise. They are beyond all encomium, whether cooked *à la française*, or jugged, or simply boiled: whichever you prefer so long as their dainty scent and taste remain unimpaired. It seems almost unkind to eat them otherwise than by themselves, but the sweetest suffers no harm from a well-chosen companionship, and a foil often enhances the loveliest beauty. A word in season must be spoken in praise of *flageolets*, those palest of pale green beans which France now offers us. Their delicate flavour imparts a new loveliness to veal or chicken, and a purée made from them is indescribably attractive. At the other end of the scale green corn should now be obtainable for our American visitors, but it provides a dish rather

95

sickly sweet for our British palates, I fancy. Cucumbers must be mentioned here, not so much for themselves as for a summery amalgamation with veal. Cook some thin *escalopes* in butter, and to the butter and veal juices add, after the cutlets have been removed, a good cupful of cream, salt and pepper and a pinch of paprika. Stir this all well together and boil quickly for a few minutes till it thickens, and then add a few pieces of butter off the flame. Now pour this over the veal which you have surrounded with rounds of boiled cucumber. A really marvellous combination of contrasting flavours.

Veal Cutlets with Cucumber

Veal
Butter
Cream
Paprika
Cucumber

I must apologise for this digression, or the salad-lover will think I have forgotten him, for it is to him that the cucumber properly belongs. Now is the amateur salad-maker happy in his wider choice of cool ingredients. Dietetics apart, a salad should be eaten at some meal or other every day, if only for us to rejoice in its delicious coolness. Lettuce (the cooler, crisper cos for me!), chicory, endive, watercress, cucumber, beetroot, tomato, dandelion, batavia, corn salad, the cresses—what a host there are, beside the cooked vegetables, potatoes, French beans, cauliflower, pimentoes, and all the combinations with meat or fish or fruit or nuts! We should adventure further into these realms, for what vistas they display unimagined by most of us. Get a salad-book and see; and your friends will bless you.

And lastly, fruit. The youngling gooseberry without a pie of which no Whit Sunday (climate permitting) should be complete. And as May is especially the Empire month, to reinforce our scanty list come the Empire fruits; apples and pears, granadillas and avocado pears. (For the last, halve the pear length-

Avocado Pear Salad

wise, remove the stone, and mix the flesh in small pieces with an ordinary French dressing, serve it in the halves with a suitable cold meat, and see what it is like.) Grapes and melons and persimmons can add to the diversity of our dessert. Pomegranates, a tiresome fruit if tackled whole, can be made palatable and presentable if some large ones are halved, the seeds removed, and the halves arranged in a dish and sprinkled with rose water. Now some smaller ones must be crushed and to their juice an equal amount of water added with enough sugar to make a good syrup. Thicken this over the fire, and, when it is cool, pour it over the halves. It has a very pleasant sharpness.

As for strawberries . . . well, they are as yet but a rosy dawn of the midsummer month they usher in.

Avocado pears
Oil
Vinegar
Salt
Pepper

Compote of
Pomegranates

Pomegranates
Sugar
Rose water

*   *   *

If geography forbids us Clam Chowder, we can make a Fish Chowder instead.

Buy a small cod or haddock weighing about four pounds. Skin the fish, bone it, and cut the flesh into pieces about two inches square. Bring two cupfuls of water to the boil and cook in this the cod's head, tail and bones for twenty minutes. While this is cooking, cut a one-and-a-half-inch cube of fat salt pork into small pieces, extract the fat by frying and cook a sliced onion in the fat for five minutes. Now strain the fat into a stewpan, add to it four cupfuls of potatoes cut into three-quarter-inch cubes which have been boiled in enough water to cover them for five minutes and then drained. Add to the fat and potatoes two cupfuls of water and cook for five

Fish
Chowder

Cod or Haddock
Fat salt pork
Onion
Potatoes
Milk

minutes. Now pour in the liquor from the bones and put in the pieces of fish. Cover and simmer for ten minutes when you add four cupfuls of scalded milk, a tablespoonful of salt, an eighth of a tablespoonful of pepper and three tablespoonfuls of butter. Bring to the boil, simmer a little longer and serve.

The unfamiliar aspect of this recipe is due to its being a transcription from an American one.

Spring
Vegetable
Soup

Carrots
Turnips
Leeks
Cabbage
Lettuce
Peas
Chervil
Stock
Egg

Now is the time for a Spring Vegetable Soup.

Scrape some young carrots and turnips and cut them in thin slices, also the white part of two leeks treated in the same way, and the heart of a young cabbage cut in four. Cook these slowly in butter in a covered saucepan till they are tender. Then add a quartered lettuce heart, a handful of fresh peas and a little chervil chopped up, and finally enough stock to serve your purpose when the soup has been reduced by a third. This you now do on a slow fire (it will take a good time), and just before you are ready for it—practically on its way from the saucepan to the tureen—mix well in with it the beaten yolk of an egg.

Lettuce Soup

Lettuces
Spinach
Parsley
Water
Egg

Lettuce Soup is equally spring-like, but much easier.

Cut two lettuces and a handful of spinach into strips, and cook them in butter with a handful of parsley coarsely chopped, till they are all quite soft. Add hot water, salt and pepper, bring to the boil and simmer for about three-quarters of an hour. Before serving add a beaten yolk of an egg to this soup, too, and be sure that the parsley stalks, and the hard parts of the lettuce and spinach leaves, have been discarded, or the soup will be stringy.

MAY

We can still bake some potatoes in their jackets, so let us do so now, with a little difference. Cut off a piece of their ends, scoop out their insides and make a smooth purée of it, adding a little grated cheese, if you like. Half fill each case with this, break an egg into each, moisten with a drop of cream and bake in the oven till the eggs are set.

Eggs in Potatoes

Potatoes and possibly Cheese Egg Cream

Omelettes are excellent in May, and indeed in most other months. Two suggestions for this one are to fill your omelette either with pieces of artichoke bottoms or red pimentoes warmed in butter. It is pleasant sometimes to have something out of season, and both these vegetables are almost as good in tins as they are out of the greengrocer's, if indeed he has them.

Omelette aux fonds d'artichauts or aux piments

It is Empire month, when we are urged to buy Empire goods more lavishly than in the rest of the year. Empire Salmon is one of these. No one will claim for it the admirable flavour of our own river fish, but it can be made extremely eatable if it is treated properly. One suggestion for its presentation at the most particular table is Salmon *à la Mornay*.

Salmon à la Mornay

Salmon Onion Fish stock or Water Bouquet garni Cheese Cream Lemon

Brown your slices of salmon quickly with a chopped onion in an ounce of butter. Add three-quarters of a pint of fish stock (or water, if you have no stock ready), salt, pepper, and a *bouquet* of parsley, thyme and bayleaf. Cover and simmer for about twenty minutes. When the fish is nearly done, cook a heaped tablespoonful of flour in an ounce of butter for five minutes in another pan, take out the fish and keep it warm, and make a sauce with the butter, flour and the strained liquor in which the salmon has been cooked. Bring it to the boil, simmer, and add a tablespoonful of grated Parmesan cheese, a little cream and a good squeeze of lemon juice. Season, pour over the fish, glaze if you like in the oven, and serve.

Stuffed Herrings, I

*Herrings
Parsley
Breadcrumbs
Butter
Egg
Milk*

This is a way of Stuffing Herrings which is not very well known. It deserves better acquaintance.

Split open some large herrings with soft roes, which you will remove and chop up with parsley and soft breadcrumbs. Mix well together and season with a little pepper. Now melt some butter—not too much—in a saucepan, break into it an egg, stir it, add the mixture of chopped roes, stir again so that it does not set before all is well mixed. Remove the backbones of the herrings as best you can, stuff the fish with the egg and roe, and bake them in a fire-proof dish with a little butter for nearly half an hour. They should be served with a sauce of the liquor in which they have baked stirred over the fire for a few minutes with a little milk.

Stuffed Herrings, II

*Herrings
Suet
Breadcrumbs
Parsley
Lemon
Milk*

This is another way of stuffing them.

Split them and remove their backbones. Season them with pepper and salt and spread on the inside a thin layer of forcemeat composed of one part finely chopped suet to two parts breadcrumbs, some chopped parsley and a little grated lemon rind, all mixed together and moistened with milk. Roll up the herrings from neck to tail (you should, by the way, have removed their heads and tail fins), tie or skewer each of them, pack them tightly in a buttered pie-dish, cover with buttered paper, and bake in a moderate oven for about an hour, not less.

**Sole
Red Mullet
à la meunière
à l'orange**

Oranges add a special distinction to the fish course. For example, Sole or Red Mullet *à la meunière à l'orange*, especially the Red Mullet.

Having floured the fish and fried it in butter, dish it and lay on it a row of orange sections carefully peeled and with the pips and pith removed. Warm them through, squeeze a little orange juice into the butter in which the fish was cooked, brown it lightly and pour it over. If a stronger orange taste (which I advocate) is desired, a few very thin *julienne* strips of orange peel, boiled for a few minutes to remove their bitterness, can also be added.

Sole or Red Mullet Oranges

Sole *à l'hongroise* is a simple dish and admirable for the warmer weather.

Fry in butter, without browning, a dessertspoonful of chopped onion lightly seasoned with paprika. Add three tablespoonfuls of white wine, a small cupful of fish stock (which you will have made from the trimmings of the sole) and two small tomatoes peeled and roughly chopped. Cook this together for about ten minutes. Meanwhile arrange the fillets in a buttered dish; now pour over the mixture and cook in a moderate oven till done. Take out the fillets and keep them warm, reduce the liquid in which they have been cooked till it is thick, then add a little cream and a squeeze of lemon, and pour it over them.

Sole à l'hongroise

*Onion
Paprika
White wine
Fish stock
Tomatoes
Sole
Cream
Lemon*

Lobster Pancakes are seasonable, too, and out of the ordinary.

Make some pancakes as thin as possible, using unsweetened batter, of course, and keep them warm. Toss some pieces of cooked lobster, cut fairly small, in butter; season them with paprika, and bind them with a little thick Béchamel sauce to which you have added a spoonful of tomato purée. Stuff the pancakes with this, arrange them on a long fireproof dish, cover with more Béchamel sauce, sprinkle with grated cheese and brown quickly before serving.

Lobster Pancakes, I

*Pancakes
Lobster
Paprika
Béchamel sauce
Tomato purée
Cheese*

Lobster Pancakes, II

Pancakes
Lobster
Mushrooms
Tomatoes
Truffle
Brandy
Cream

A more elaborate stuffing can be prepared by making a sauce to bind the pieces of lobster out of a few slices of mushrooms and tomatoes cooked in butter, a sliced truffle and the red part of the lobster all chopped together and mixed with a little brandy and some cream. But in this case, do not sprinkle with cheese or brown the sauce.

Fricassée of Scallops

Scallops
Béchamel sauce
Lemon
Egg
Parsley

Those first-cousins of the lobster, Scallops, make an excellent *fricassée*, if we cannot rise to a lobster. Cut the scallops in four pieces and stew them in a good white sauce for about three-quarters of an hour. A squeeze of lemon juice, the beaten yolk of an egg, and a very little chopped parsley should be stirred in at the last moment. It makes a very pretty dish, which you might well adorn with a few delicate little heaps of peas.

Beef in Lettuce Leaves, I

Beef
Rice
Egg
Milk
Lettuce
Stock

The more frequent appearance of lettuces in the shop windows should remind us of a dish which is not very often encountered in this country, though it is popular in various forms on the Continent and in the Near East, whence I fancy it hails.

This is Beef (or other meat) in Lettuce Leaves. There are many ways of preparing this. I will give two.

For the first mince a pound of raw beef, and boil a gill of rice in milk. Let the rice get cold. Beat up an egg in a little milk and add it to the rice and beef, with some pepper and salt. Take a good spoonful of the mixture and wrap it in a lettuce leaf, repeating this till you have used it all. Tie the lettuce leaves with cotton and brown them all over in butter. Cover with some good, well-flavoured stock and cook very slowly in the oven for two hours.

For the second way you will want the same quantity of minced beef. Mix it with a tablespoonful of finely chopped onion, two ounces of chopped suet, a pinch of allspice, salt and pepper. Shape the mixture into pieces about the size of a small egg. Wrap each piece in a lettuce leaf, and arrange them as closely as possible in a long fireproof dish. Cover them with stock or gravy, with a piece of buttered paper, and the lid, and cook for about half an hour.

Beef in Lettuce Leaves, II

Beef
Onion
Suet
Allspice
Lettuce
Stock or Gravy

Young cabbage leaves may be used instead of lettuce so long as they are first boiled for five minutes; or the stuffed leaves can be braised on a bed of bacon-rind, sliced carrots and onions, and a *bouquet* of parsley, thyme and bayleaf. This last is specially recommended.

Inventiveness can also be exercised in the concoction of various savoury stuffings of veal, chicken, and so on. The Americans, for instance, have a version of this dish in which the stuffing consists of half a tablespoonful of lightly fried chopped onion, a cupful of chopped cooked chicken or veal, the same of fine white breadcrumbs moistened with stock and a beaten egg, salt and pepper. They serve this kind of lettuce roll with a tomato sauce poured round it.

Veal or Chicken in Lettuce Leaves

Onion
Chicken or Veal
Breadcrumbs
Stock
Egg
Lettuce
Tomato sauce

When you are tired of all the usual ways of presenting Lamb Cutlets, the Swedish fashion may appeal to you.

Swedish Lamb Cutlets

Sprinkle the cutlets with minced onions and shallots, parsley, thyme and bayleaf, the juice of a lemon and a few drops of oil. Marinade them thus for half an hour, turning them once or twice. Then dry them, brush them over with melted butter, cover them with fine breadcrumbs, and grill them.

Lamb cutlets
Onions
Shallots
Parsley
Thyme
Bayleaf
Lemon
Oil

Butter
Breadcrumbs
Apples
White wine
Horseradish

Meanwhile you have peeled and sliced half a pound of apples and stewed them quickly to a purée with a little white wine (the wine could be omitted). Just before dishing up, stir into this purée two good tablespoonfuls of grated horseradish. Pour it into the centre of the dish and serve the cutlets round it.

Roast Lamb
French fashion

Lamb
Potatoes
Onions
Carrots
and possibly
Garlic

There is a good deal to be said for the French method of roasting a joint of lamb, which is to do so on a bed of sliced potatoes, onions and carrots well mixed together. The disadvantage is that all your dripping is absorbed by the vegetables, but they are very delicious, and this way of cooking imparts an entrancing flavour to the cold meat. Garlic is also added in most parts of France, either inserted near the bone, or a little chopped very finely and put in the bottom of the dish. I am told that the after effects of the latter method are less potent !

Kahab
Sauté of Veal)

Veal Cutlet
Caraway seeds
Onion
Lemon
Sour cream

An alternative recipe to the Veal with cucumber is an Austrian dish called *Kahab*, a different form of a *sauté*.

Cut about a pound of veal cutlet into pieces about the size of a matchbox. Put a good piece of butter into an earthenware casserole or stewpan, melt it and add the meat seasoned with salt and pepper, a quarter of a teaspoonful of caraway seeds (in a muslin bag), a very small onion and half a lemon both very thinly sliced. Fry all this for about ten minutes, not too fast, then add half a pint of sour cream, put on the lid and cook slowly in a moderate oven for about three-quarters of an hour.

Fritto Misto
of Meat

Veal cutlet

A *Fritto Misto* of Fruit was suggested for January, or indeed for any other month. The orthodox *Fritto Misto* of Meat consists of all or any of the following: veal cutlet, calf's liver, calf or lamb sweetbread, veal or sheep's kidney, an aubergine or artichoke, brains, and a cauliflower. The latter must, of course, be parboiled. All these ingredients you cut into thin slices (the cauliflower into flowerets), season them and dip them in melted butter and flour. They should then be *sauté-d* in separate pans in plenty of butter, the juice of a lemon squeezed into the mingled butter after they are cooked, and this sauce poured over the pieces, which should be served very hot. Or, if it is preferred, they can all be fried very crisply in oil. In any case, the dish should be garnished with lemons.

*Calf's liver
Calf or Lamb
sweetbread
Veal or Sheep's
kidney
Aubergine or
Artichoke
Brains
Cauliflower
Lemon*

We have discussed Spring Chicken already, but not in a fried fashion. This is a way they have of cooking him in the Southern States of America. It is perfectly simple, as you would expect, but very good indeed.

American
Fried Chicken

*Chicken
Pork fat
and possibly
Milk and Cream*

Cut a young chicken in pieces, wash them in cold water, drain them, but do not wipe them dry. Now sprinkle them with salt and pepper and coat them as thickly as possible with flour, pressing it well on. Then fry them in plenty of salt pork fat till they are well browned and tender. They are usually served with a plain white sauce made of half milk and half cream.

Another American way of cooking chicken is to cut it up in pieces which are then salted and peppered and rolled in egg and breadcrumbs. Do not fry them, but put them in a well-greased baking-dish and bake them for half an hour in a hot oven. After they have been cooking for five minutes they should be basted with melted butter. A white sauce is also served with these.

American
Baked
Chicken

*Chicken
Egg and
breadcrumbs*

Vol-au-vent

Vol-au-vent cases can be bought from most pastry-cooks, if you do not want to take the trouble of making them yourself. As a matter of fact, for the ordinary cook, these are one of the few things which are better bought. They are, in any case, extremely useful, for a most attractive course can always be prepared with their help. Any kind of white meat, cut into small pieces and combined with mushrooms or other meats such as ham and tongue in a delicate sauce can be used for fillings, as can cold pieces of fish or shellfish bound with an appropriate sauce. Put them in the oven with their savoury contents and put on the little top a trifle jauntily, for the *vol-au-vent*, as its name betrays, is a slightly frivolous form of food. There are many times, however, when it has come to the rescue of the harassed housewife racking her brains for something new for her 'in-laws', which will be attractive but not extravagant!

Chicken
Vol-au-vent
*Cooked
Chicken
Ham
or Tongue
Mushrooms
Truffles
Béchamel sauce
Aromatic spice*

Your own ingenuity will devise various fillings. Here are one or two for your guidance.

First, with chicken: that is small cubes of cooked chicken and ham or tongue, slices of mushrooms (the little bottled ones are best for this), and truffles, all mixed with a thick Béchamel sauce, flavoured with salt, pepper and aromatic spice.

Vegetable
Vol-au-vent
*Cooked
cauliflower
Cheese
Cream sauce or
Mushroom
sauce*

Second, with vegetables: for instance, a mixture of cooked cauliflower and grated cheese and a good cream or mushroom sauce.

Vol-au-vent à
la financière

Third, more for curiosity's sake, because the *Vol-au-vent à la financière* is the one most commonly served in restaurants, though I doubt if the ingredients are always correctly used: truffles cooked in Madeira, a brown sauce made with good stock, little pieces of mushrooms, *fonds d'artichauts, quen-*

elles, and to give it some substance, however airy, little bits of sweetbread cooked in butter.

Asparagus cannot always be eaten plainly, however much we may be addicted to it; but if it is, we might take a tip from the Belgians. It is often heartbreaking for many of us to have to leave the delicious melted butter on our plates after we have sucked the last fragrant drops from the asparagus. A sensible Flemish custom is to serve each guest with half the hot yolk of a hard-boiled egg, which is then crushed and used with the butter. Or the egg and butter can be mixed beforehand—in the proportion of half an egg yolk to two tablespoonfuls of butter —seasoned and served with the asparagus.

Asparagus Butter with Egg

The Polish garnish which we have encountered with *petits poussins* is well adapted to asparagus. After you have dished the asparagus, well drained, sprinkle the tips with hot hard-boiled egg yolk and finely chopped parsley, and throw over it at the last moment some fresh breadcrumbs which have been made golden in butter when it is just foaming.

Asparagus à la Polonaise

*Asparagus
Hard-boiled egg
Parsley
Breadcrumbs*

Mushrooms stuffed with fish are a good savoury or luncheon dish. Lightly fry as many mushrooms as you want (they should be fairly large, but not too coarse), and heap upon them a mixture of their stalks chopped up and tossed in butter, some parsley, a tiny bit of garlic (or onion) and the remains of any cold fish you have by you, all mixed together and bound with the yolk of an egg. Sprinkle with breadcrumbs, dot with butter and bake for about a quarter of an hour. Serve on toast or fried bread.

Mushrooms Stuffed with Fish

*Mushrooms
Parsley
Garlic or
Onion
Cold fish
Egg
Breadcrumbs*

Imported new potatoes do not taste much, so we can make this experiment with them. Half cook

Potatoes with Lemon

New potatoes
Lemon
Butter
Parsley

some small new potatoes, and pour the water away, except just enough to cover them. Into this squeeze the juice of a lemon and finish cooking. Drain them well, and pour over melted butter, sprinkling them as they leave the kitchen with chopped parsley.

Granadilla or
Passion Fruit
Cream

Granadilla pulp
Sugar
Lemon
Cream
Gelatine

Pomegranates have already reminded us of Empire sweets. Granadilla Cream is another unusual flavour which should become popular. As far as I can gather, Granadillas and Passion Fruit are to all intents and purposes the same. They both come from South Africa, and Australia too, and the pulp is imported in tins. You may prefer to rub the pulp through a sieve again, as it is populated by little black seeds which, however decorative they are, may not invariably meet with favour.

To make the Cream, add to the pulp, sieved or not, a tablespoonful of fine sugar and a teaspoonful of lemon juice, and let it stand in a covered basin for about three-quarters of an hour. Stiffly whip up half a pint of cream, fold it lightly into the pulp, then stir in two ounces of gelatine which you have dissolved in a little hot water. Mould it and let it get cool, and serve iced, if possible.

Golden Berries

The Granadilla pulp gives an additional and pleasant flavour to fruit salads, and by the way, do not forget also to order a tin of Golden Berries, which are our old friends, the Cape Gooseberries (once in their dried state so universally, and unfortunately, decorative) masquerading charmingly as an eatable.

Lemon Pie

Pastry
Cornflour

Canada gives us Lemon Pie. All the really lovable old Mommas on the Pictures make a pie of some kind, and I am sure that Lemon Pie is a favourite !

MAY

Make a *flan* case of puff pastry, baking till three-quarters done. Meanwhile mix a dessertspoonful of cornflour with a little milk till it is smooth, boil a pint of milk and pour it over the cornflour, stirring well. Now add an ounce of sugar, the finely grated rind of a lemon and the yolks of three eggs, and stir on a low heat till the mixture thickens. Pour this into the *flan* case. Beat the egg whites as stiffly as possible, stir six ounces of castor sugar lightly into the froth and spread it on top of the pie, which you will now bake in a moderate oven till the méringue is crisp and golden.

Some Momma!

Milk
Lemon
Eggs

The Angels having flown with the oysters, Devils on Horseback are now the order of the day. These are our tiny friends, the thin rolls of bacon, each stuffed with a stoned French plum in which has been inserted a peeled Jordan almond tossed in butter and seasoned with salt, paprika and cayenne. A different Devil is a stuffing of a good piece of chicken's liver sprinkled with finely chopped onion and parsley, salt, pepper, and cayenne. Tie or skewer the little rolls, and grill or bake them in the oven. Serve on toast, very hot.

Devils on Horseback, I

Bacon
French plums
Almonds
Paprika and Cayenne

These little rolls are often a godsend—like the *vol-au-vent*—for they can be filled with all kinds of stuffings, and have been known to tempt the most difficult palate even in the dog-days.

Devils on Horseback, II

Bacon
Chicken's liver
Onion
Parsley
Cayenne

JUNE

THE FOOD OF THE MONTH

Food which is in season all the year round is given in the table on page 19.

Note.—Newcomers are printed in italics.

FISH

Sea Fish

Hake	Herrings
Mackerel	Whitebait

River Fish

Eels   Salmon
Trout

Shell Fish

Crabs   Scallops

MEAT

Lamb

POULTRY

Ducklings   Guinea-fowl

GAME

Buck Venison

VEGETABLES

Jerusalem Artichokes
Asparagus   *Aubergine*
Cauliflower   Green Corn
Green Peas   Horseradish
New Potatoes   Seakale
Spinach
Spring Onions
Watercress

FRUIT

Apricots   *Cherries*
Green Gooseberries
Melons   *Raspberries*
Strawberries

EMPIRE IMPORTED FRESH FRUIT

Apples	Granadillas
Grapes	Grape Fruit
Limes	Naartjes
Oranges	Pears

The following recipes are given during this month:

June for jubilation! For now Mother Earth almost embarrasses us with her riches, and the gastronomic year enters upon its most glorious stage. With what profusion she flings out the plenitude of garden and field, and with what cunning she sets her offerings before us, so that every mood is suited:—and most of all her triumphs, tender peas and new potatoes, luscious lettuces, rosy cherries nodding on the bough, strawberries blushing on their fresh-strown bed, red and ivory spilth of raspberries sheltering under the dewy leaves. It is easy to be lyrical about June. Let us emulate our greedy childhood days, and rob her orchards and kitchen-gardens for all we are worth.

We have no regrets. We shall hardly miss the savoury Smelt, though he is light and toothsome;

June, the lavish month of garden and field, provides the gourmand's most paradisal days

JUNE

Eel Matelote

Eels
Red wine
Onion
Bouquet garni
Garlic
Brandy
Butter
Flour

for all the other fish are here for us, the eel included
fresh from his Atlantic voyage. *Matelote* is the
famous way of eating him. Cut him in sections and
boil him in a pint of red wine with a minced onion
a *bouquet* of parsley, thyme and bayleaf, two cloves o
garlic, a pinch of salt and four peppercorns. Whe
it is boiling add three tablespoonfuls of burn
brandy. Cover and cook till the fish is done, whe
you take them out and keep them warm. Strain th
liquor and reduce it by a third, thicken it with
paste of butter and flour and pour it over the eels
(The quantities are for two pounds of fish.)

For those to whom jellied eels partake too much o
the eating-house, there are several ways of preparin
him as a cold *hors d'œuvre*: with white wine and pap
rika, with white wine and herbs, or with herbs an
beer in the Flemish fashion.

As for meat, Lamb goes on from strength t
strength and Veal is at its best, while for those wh
want a touch of gaminess Buck Venison is to b
had—not so good as the doe later on, by any means
but for cooler days a *civet* can be made of it in th
same way as of hare. Chickens are a tower o
strength for picnic days, and with hams and tongue

Guinea-fowl

will grace many an alfresco meal. Guinea-fowl is no
to be despised, and can be treated in the man
culinary manners that apply to pheasant, which wil
lend attraction to his rather dryish flesh. Ducklings
rising from their beds of new peas, now await th
shipments of oranges which South Africa is sendin
us. Braise the duckling in a third of a pint of brow
sauce and double that amount of Espagnole sauce
When it is done—and it must be well done—re
move it and reduce the sauce till it is stiff, the
squeeze into it the juice of two oranges and half

**Duckling
braised with
Oranges**

Duckling
Brown sauce

lemon. At the last minute throw in some thin *julienne* strips of half a lemon and half an orange skin, previously boiled for five minutes. Garnish with slices or segments of raw orange. You will never stuff a duckling with sage and onion again.

Espagnole sauce
Oranges
Lemon

New peas are more plentiful and Cornish new potatoes should be soon here—at last the authentic flavour. By the way, why is it that we never seem to get nowadays the real delicious waxy taste of the new potatoes of our childhood? They all seem to taste alike, whether they come from Africa or Spain or France or from home. Is some horrid process of standardisation taking place, which in the end will rob us of our most dearly treasured flavours? Vanish the thought, and let us console ourselves with a truly excellent blend of early summer vegetable, new peas and young carrots *à la Nivernaise*. Melt four and a half ounces of butter in a saucepan, and put in a pound and a half of shelled peas, half a dozen spring onions, double that number of young carrots sliced in rounds, the hearts of three lettuces, a quarter of a pint of water, a lump of sugar and salt. Cover and cook gently till the vegetables are done. Reduce half a pint of cream till it is thick, and put the peas into it just before serving. Pour this into a dish and arrange the other vegetables round it.

Peas and Carrots Nivernaise

New peas
New carrots
Spring onions
Lettuce
Butter
Cream

Cauliflower perks up this month. He suffers from an inferiority complex, because he has never had a chance to be, and look, anything but plain and dull. But there are so many pretty ways of dressing him, that we might give him a little sympathy this summer and show him to our friends as attractively as possible. The French, the Italians and the Poles have all special ways of treating him, and we should take

Cauliflower
Purée à la
Dubarry

*Cauliflower
Potatoes
Cream
Butter*

a leaf out of their cookery-books. Just one, for example, a purée *à la Dubarry*, as simple as it is exciting. Cook the cauliflower in salted water, drain it and rub it through a hair sieve. Mix this purée with a quarter of its amount of potatoes mashed with cream. See that it is not too wet, heat it up, add a little butter at the last, and serve.

Lettuces have lost their imported dankness and at last blossom proudly like great green roses on our greengrocers' shelves. The elegant cos proffers its crisp and water-cool leaves; cool, too, the cresses and cucumbers for the sultry days when appetites languish. This month, too, there comes to us one of whom we must make a friend, if it is not a friend

Aubergine

already, the succulent Aubergine, that shiny, bluish object for some obscure reason called in English the Egg-Plant, which looks so thoroughly uneatable and yet is so delicious. Whether fried in rounds, or baked stuffed with egg and cheese, or in the Provençal fashion or, more solidly, *à l'égyptienne*, with onion, tomato, and chopped mutton, it is a momentous and indescribable experience; and can even become an obsession. I make no excuse for insisting on its acquaintance. You will find out the reason for yourself, if you take my advice.

And now we come to June's great gifts. Melons, for their own sweet savour or for the enclosure of fruit salads as icy as themselves; the Apricot, a rarity, alas! save as a visitor from other shores; and Naartjes, those super-tangerines from South Africa. But none as sweet and as delicate as our own darlings—cherries, raspberries, strawberries—so delicious in their first appearance that we shall eat them fresh and raw. It may be doubted whether the schoolboy's mash of raspberries or strawberries and cream yields place to any invention of the epicure, and yet ... for airy lightness there is much to be said for half a pound of fresh raspberries well whipped up with the same quantity of castor sugar and the white of an egg, an ambrosial blend. And there are those who swear by Strawberries *au Kirsch* as their happiest summer experience. We can but try them. Cut a pound of strawberries in halves. Whip up some cream with sugar, adding a liqueur-glassful of Kirsch, and half a dozen or so squashed strawberries to give it colour. Sprinkle the strawberries with sugar and mix them well with the cream. Curaçao or Grand Marnier could be used instead of Kirsch, if preferred, and a good dash of any of these liqueurs to ordinary strawberries and cream has many devotees.

Strawberries au Kirsch

Strawberries Cream Kirsch

And if the weather is wet, and the berries look a little dishevelled for a proper appearance at dessert, do not let us despise the help of an orange or two by mixing the juice of two of them with a purée made by passing a pound of strawberries through a hair sieve and adding the requisite amount of sugar. This purée makes a regal bed for the more presentable berries which you have, of course, put aside.

Strawberries with Orange, I

Strawberries Oranges

And lastly, another combination. Scoop out some halved oranges. Remove the pips and pith from the flesh (and do not lose the juice), mix this with some crushed strawberries, a few stoned cherries, castor sugar and a few drops of maraschino, and refill the orange halves.

And jubilate!

Strawberries with Orange, II

Strawberries Oranges Cherries Maraschino

*   *   *

Cucumber Soup

Cucumbers
Vinegar
Butter
White stock
Breadcrumbs
Milk
Onions
Sugar
Cream

Cucumber Soup makes a very good introduction to a June dinner.

Peel two cucumbers, cut them into small pieces, remove the seeds, and boil the pieces for three minutes in some water to which you have added a dash of vinegar. Drain them well and put them into a saucepan with four ounces of butter. When that has melted, add two pints of white stock, a coffee-cupful of fine white breadcrumbs soaked in milk, two onions cut up small, salt, and a pinch of sugar. Bring this to the boil, simmer a little while, stirring occasionally. Strain the soup when it is done, and just before serving stir in four or five, or more, tablespoonfuls of cream.

Spanish Omelette, II

Potato
Tomato
Onion
Pimento
and possibly
Parsley

A different Spanish Omelette from that which I described in April can be made as follows:

Cut a potato in small cubes and fry in butter. In a separate pan fry also in butter a peeled tomato, an onion and a red pepper (pimento) finely chopped. Pour your omelette mixture into the pan, add these ingredients, season all fairly highly, and cook the omelette like a pancake, tossing it once. Serve flat, with a sprinkling of parsley if you like.

Œufs mollets

Œufs mollets, or peeled soft-boiled eggs, make a welcome change for summer meals. They take six minutes, no more, to cook from the time the water in which they have been plunged has come to the boil again. They should then be left for a minute or two in cold water and carefully shelled. They can be kept warm, if desired, in moderately salted hot water.

Various ways of serving them will at once occur to you. For instance, all the garnishes for poached eggs (spinach, asparagus tips or purée, endives, peas *la française*) can equally well be applied to them, or they can be coated with various sauces, Soubise, Béchamel, Mornay, Tomato, Robert, and so on. In hot weather they certainly have a less forbidding appearance than poached eggs, and there is always the element of surprise about them for the uninitiated.

A *Fritto Misto* of Fish is our last variation on this theme.

Fritto Misto of Fish

Any small fish

Any small fish could be used to compile a very charming gastronomic comment on a warm midday or evening: very small slip soles or other little flat fish, tiny whiting, prawns, pieces of lobster, whitebait—all these and others could be employed to assemble a light summer dish which, after its ingredients have been rolled in egg and breadcrumbs and fried, should certainly be accompanied by some beautifully green fried parsley.

Before Mackerel and Green Gooseberries both disappear, we should eat them in conjunction.

Mackerel with Gooseberry Sauce

Mackerel White wine or Vinegar Fennel Gooseberries Sugar

Cut the mackerel in three, crosswise, and boil them in a *court-bouillon* of wine or vinegar, to which you have added a pinch of fennel if you can get it. Don't be discouraged by this instruction, for the fish can also be boiled in water and vinegar, though they will, of course, then lack the finer flavour which the *court-bouillon* imparts.) Drain the pieces and skin them, and serve them with a sauce made by cooking a pound of green gooseberries with three ounces of sugar in just enough water to cover them. When the fruit is done, rub through a hair sieve, and add this new combination of flavours to your gastronomic repertoire.

Sole *Villeroi* is more suitable for a special occasion.

Sole Villeroi

JUNE

Mushrooms
Parsley
Shallots or
Onions
Fillets of Sole
Milk
Cream
Fish stock
Breadcrumbs

Toss in an ounce of butter half a dozen mushrooms finely chopped, a tablespoonful of chopped parsley and two of minced shallots or onions. When they are cooked, let them get cold. Have some fillets of sole ready, spread some of the mixture on each, roll them up, tie with cotton, arrange in a buttered *sauté* pan and cook for ten minutes. Now have some little china cases ready, and into each put a rolled fillet with a small mushroom on top, filling up the case with a good white sauce made with milk, cream, and a little fish stock made from the trimmings of the sole. Sprinkle each with a few breadcrumbs, and brown quickly in the oven.

Anchovy
Cream of
Turbot

Turbot
Breadcrumbs
Milk
Worcester sauce
Ground mace
Cayenne
Cream
Eggs
Peas
Cream sauce
Anchovy
essence

Anchovy Cream of Turbot is a decorative dish for a dinner-party.

Pass a pound of turbot through a sieve, and mix it with a teaspoonful of breadcrumbs soaked in milk and well drained, half a teaspoonful of Worcester sauce, the same of salt, a pinch of ground mace, a sprinkle of cayenne, and a cupful of good cream. Whip up the whites of four eggs and fold them into this mixture. Pour it into a buttered *soufflé* mould and cook for twenty minutes. Serve surrounded with green peas and covered with a rich cream sauce well flavoured with anchovy essence.

Lobster à la
Newburg, I

Lobster
Madeira
Cream
Egg
Rice

The horrors of cutting up live lobsters to make Lobster *à la Newburg* are avoided by this simple method, which gives very satisfactory results.

Chop up the meat of a medium-sized lobster, and fry it in an ounce of butter in a stewpan, seasoning it well. Then add enough Madeira nearly to cover the pieces, and let it reduce almost entirely. Add to this half a pint of cream and a beaten egg yolk, and let it thicken. Serve very hot with a little rice.

A simpler way, without the use of wine, is to warm up the pieces of lobster in butter, and to add to them a mixture of two egg yolks, half a gill of thick cream, a few drops of onion juice, a salt-spoonful of salt, the same of Krona pepper and a trifle of nutmeg. Stir till the mixture thickens, and serve at once.

Lobster à la Newburg, II

Lobster
Eggs
Cream
Onion juice
Krona pepper
Nutmeg

A remarkable dish can be prepared from Beef and New Peas. Like so many really first-class dishes, this is extremely easy to make.

Take a nice piece of steak, salt and pepper it and brown it in butter in a casserole for about ten minutes, turning it so that the meat is 'closed' all over. Now just add some fresh-shelled peas (they should be all about the same size, and the smaller the better), a little more salt and pepper, put on the lid and simmer very gently for two and a half or three hours. As a result of this masterly inattention you will obtain a marvellous mixture of beef, butter and peas, the exquisite flavours of each having entered into the other. And don't, by the way, begrudge the beef, which is very eatable indeed when cold.

Beef Braised with New Peas

Steak
Peas

I have already advocated Lamb roast *à la française*. To cook the joint *en cocotte* is also a pleasing method. Put it in the *cocotte* with some lightly fried young carrots and turnips, a few button onions and a couple of glasses of dry white wine. Or stock can be used by those who do not like the taste of wine. When the joint is cooked, add a little cream and chopped parsley to the gravy before serving.

Lamb en cocotte

Lamb
Carrots
Turnips
Onions
White wine or Stock
Cream
Parsley

An unusual way of serving veal cutlets is to egg-and-breadcrumb and fry them, and dish them up round a fine purée of turnips.

Veal Cutlets with Turnips

Veal Kidney

Veal Kidney makes an admirable dish, and is often liked by those who find the flavour of sheep's kidney too strong. It can be cooked in many ways, sliced or whole; plainly with butter in a casserole; in the same way with the addition of *fines herbes*; with pieces of blanched bacon, mushrooms and tiny onions, or cut in slices and grilled on a skewer. When it is plainly cooked it can with advantage be served with a dryish purée of tomatoes and with tomatoes stuffed with forcemeat or *petits pois* surrounding it.

Veal Kidney à la Liègoise

Veal kidney
Gin
Juniper berries

But the best way of all, to my thinking, is to cook it whole in butter in a casserole, and just before serving to throw in a wineglassful of burnt gin and a few crushed juniper berries. This is quite wonderful, and if you can get the berries fresh from your own or a friend's garden, so much the better. Otherwise they can be obtained in bottles, but they should be well crushed.

Chicken Bonne Femme

Chicken
Pickled pork
Potatoes
and possibly
Veal gravy

The following is a very simple but most exquisite fashion of cooking a chicken, preferably a spring chicken. Blanch, by boiling for a few minutes, two or three slices of breast of pickled pork. Cut them in pieces and fry them in a little butter. Take them out and fry the chicken all over in the same fat. Having done this, put it into a cocotte with the pieces of pork and the fat in which it has been fried but first you will have fried lightly in that fat about three-quarters of a pound of potatoes cut into not too thin rounds. Put these round the chicken, cover the cocotte and cook in the oven for about an hour. Serve in the cocotte. The addition of a few tablespoonfuls of veal gravy at the end is a pleasant, but not absolutely necessary, extra.

JUNE

Pigeons _à la Tartare_ are easy enough to prepare.
Get the poulterer to spatchcock them. Sprinkle
them with melted butter, then with breadcrumbs
pressed well on, and grill them very carefully. Serve
them, as their name implies, with a Tartare sauce.

Here are three ways of serving asparagus.
One. Cook some asparagus tips and drain them
well. Melt a piece of butter in a saucepan, add a
cupful of cream, salt, pepper and a grating of nutmeg. Mix well together till boiling, add the asparagus tips, and cook on till the cream reduces and
thickens.

Two. Cook the asparagus, drain it and dish it up
flat. Coat the heads with a little Mornay sauce,
sprinkle with a little grated Parmesan cheese, cover
the stalks with buttered paper and brown the heads
quickly under the grill.

Three. This is rather a novelty. Cook the asparagus till nearly done. Cut off the tips, not too shortly,
and put them into cold water. Drain them and let
them dry. Now roll them in flour and tie a few together in little bundles. Dip these in beaten egg and
fry in deep fat till golden. The small thin asparagus
(sprew) is perhaps best for this dish.

An Italian recipe for serving Cauliflower will be
appreciated by those who are rather tired of the
everlasting cauliflower with plain white sauce.
Fry a small onion and two boned anchovies
chopped very fine in some butter. Add to this half
a pint of stock, a teaspoonful of mixed herbs, and a
dash of vinegar, thickening with a little flour if you
wish. Pour this unusual sauce over the boiled or
steamed cauliflower.

Pigeons à la Tartare
Pigeons
Butter
Breadcrumbs
Tartare sauce

Asparagus à la Crème
Asparagus
Cream
Nutmeg

Asparagus au Gratin
Asparagus
Mornay sauce
Parmesan

Asparagus Fritters
Asparagus
Egg

Cauliflower Italian fashion
Onion
Anchovies
Stock
Mixed herbs
Vinegar
Cauliflower

Jugged Peas

Peas
Butter
Sugar
Mint
Black pepper

Peas are sometimes inclined to be temperamental and, however wisely we charm them, emerge hard after cooking. Jugging them has been found to obviate this distressing difficulty. Put the peas, which should be of much the same size, in a jar with a screw top or in anything with a closely fitting lid. With them put a tablespoonful of butter, a salt-spoonful of salt, a teaspoonful of castor sugar, a dozen mint leaves and a suspicion of black pepper. Put the covered vessel in a saucepan of boiling water which reaches half-way up, and boil quickly for half an hour. If the peas are old, they may take a little longer; but in any case this treatment works wonders.

Bananas au Rhum

Bananas
Demerara
sugar
Lemon
Rum
Cream

Bananas and Rum make a good combination. Try it.

Peel as many bananas as are required, and bake them, either whole or cut in half lengthwise in two or three tablespoonfuls of water, sprinkled with demerara sugar and the juice of a lemon. After they have cooked for ten minutes, throw over them a wineglassful of rum. Serve hot or cold with whipped cream, which you can flavour, if you think fit, with lemon juice or some more rum.

Apple and Greengage Mould

Apples
Greengage jelly
Cream

Apple and Greengage Jelly is a nice way of using a packet jelly. Cook a pound of peeled, cored and sliced apples in two ounces of sugar and a gill of water boiled together till they are tender. Whip them up with a fork till they are smooth and frothy, and then dissolve in this froth a pint packet of Chivers' greengage jelly cut into very small pieces. Pour this into a mould and let it set. When it is cold serve decorated with whipped cream.

Orange and Sherry Cream

Here is a pleasant Cream made with Oranges and Sherry.

JUNE

Soak an ounce of gelatine in a little cold milk. Boil up a pint of milk, and add to it the yolks of four eggs, half an orange rind finely grated, five ounces of sugar and a quarter of a pound of macaroons. Stir till it thickens, when you must add the gelatine and half a wineglassful of sherry. Strain, cool and mix in some cream and a few glacé cherries cut in small bits. Pour into a mould and serve cold.

Gelatine
Milk
Eggs
Orange
Macaroons
Sherry
Cream
Glacé cherries

While we are on the subject of oranges, a simple Orange *Soufflé* can be quickly prepared by whipping up some whites of eggs to a stiff froth, adding castor sugar and orange juice. You could, of course, flavour such a mixture with any other fruit juice, strawberry, lemon, or with chocolate or coffee. (This should perhaps strictly be called a *mousse*, but it is a dish which is usually known under the former name.)

Orange
Soufflé

Eggs
Sugar
Oranges

A light savoury, or egg course, suitable for this month can be made by beating up an egg with a gill of cream, or milk, salt, pepper and a dessertspoonful of grated cheese, a mixture of Gruyère and Parmesan being the best. Beat for a few minutes, pour into little *cocottes* and bake in a hot oven for ten minutes. Serve very quickly before the *soufflés* have time to sink. This quantity is really enough for two.

Little Cheese
Soufflés

Egg
Cream
or Milk cheese

Two elegant extras, which will help to make June meals more appetising, are *Grissini* and *Brioches*. The first, those long sticks of bread which we have enjoyed so much in Italian restaurants, are very easy to make, and have been known to keep the most fidgety eater quite quiet.

Mix half a pound of flour, half an ounce of butter, a saltspoonful of baking powder and a pinch of salt

Grissini
Flour

Butter
Baking powder
Water
possibly Milk or
Egg

with boiling water in a basin, but see that the mixture is not too moist. Knead it out till it is quite smooth, then roll it into sticks about eight or nine inches long and about the same thickness as an ordinary lead pencil. Bake these in a fairly slow oven till they are quite hard and a golden biscuit colour. If you like you can paint a little milk over them, or some beaten egg, before baking.

Brioches

Flour
Yeast
Water
Salt
Sugar
Milk
Butter
Eggs

The second extra we have all loved at the pastry-cook's; but sometimes shops are distant, or they have no *Brioches* ready. In that case it is always simpler to have one's own supply. This is quite an easy recipe, too, but like many good things it demands a little trouble—which, of course, no *Brioche*-lover will refuse.

Sift a pound of flour. Hollow a quarter of it and put in a quarter of an ounce of fresh yeast. Mix together with enough tepid water to make a soft paste, roll it in a ball, make a right-angled slit in the top, put it in a basin, cover it and leave it in a fairly warm place, to make the leaven.

Make a hollow in the remainder of the flour, and put in a quarter of an ounce of salt, an ounce and a half of sugar melted in two tablespoonfuls of milk, four ounces of butter, and four eggs. Mix from the centre, and then knead well for a few minutes. Hollow, add another egg, mix, knead again for two minutes, and add and mix in a final egg, six in all. Spread out the paste and lay thinly on it six ounces of butter softened to the same consistency, and work this in in small portions till it is thoroughly mixed.

Now turn the paste over and spread the leaven (which should by now be twice its original size) upon it. Mix it well, put the whole into a basin, cover it, and leave it in a temperate room for five or six hours. At the end of this time it should be turned out on to a floured board and beaten with the flat of the hand. Return it to the basin, let it ferment for another six hours, take it out, beat it again, and it is then ready to be baked in the ordinary way.

We need no longer sigh on languid mornings for a Continental breakfast, as many do.

JULY

THE FOOD OF THE MONTH

Food which is in season all the year round is given in the table on page 19.

Note.—Newcomers are printed in italics.

FISH

Sea Fish

Hake   Herrings
Mackerel   Whitebait

River Fish

Eels   Salmon
      Trout

Shell Fish

Crabs

MEAT

Lamb

POULTRY

Ducklings Guinea-fowl

GAME

Buck Venison

VEGETABLES

Globe Artichokes
Asparagus   Aubergines
Broad Beans Cauliflower
Green Corn   Green Peas
New Potatoes *Runner Beans*
  Shallots   Spinach
  Vegetable Marrows

FRUIT

Apricots   Cherries
Currants   *Figs*
Gooseberries Melons
Raspberries   Strawberries

EMPIRE IMPORTED FRESH FRUIT

Apples   Grape Fruit
Limes   Naartjes
Pears   Oranges

The following recipes are given during this month:

A friend of mine once said that while June reminded him of a nice young housewife proudly yet a little nervously entertaining him, July was like one of those hostesses who overwhelm and embarrass us by the prodigality of their kindness. There is a good deal of truth in the comparison, for whereas July possesses all the advantages and delights of June, she offers us even more, as witness the local flower-shows with their unbelievable exhibits, uneatable enlargements of our familiar food. But alas! the summer diminishes rather than increases our capacity for enjoyment. It is perhaps a little ironic that the warmer the days become and the more our zest for eating declines, the more prolific are our farms and

The multi-tudinous riches of July strive to outvie the plenitude of June

gardens and the more magnificent and profuse is the gourmand's choice. Still, July is a gastronomic paradise.

To turn to prosy facts, scallops leave us, and so does seakale, the only absentees. But both our vegetable and fruit lists are enlarged. *Mousses, soufflés,* and the lighter forms of fish are now the order of the day. For a Sunday supper, when tennis or the river has kept us late out of doors, this West Indian *Marinade* (how much prettier and more decent a word than 'souse') may be appreciated. Boil two pounds of hake, for instance, and let it get cold. Skin and bone it and put a layer in the dish in which it will be served. On this put some very thin slices of raw onion and pimentoes (which can be bought in tins if the fresh are unobtainable), a bayleaf, one or two cloves, red pepper, freshly ground black pepper and salt. Sprinkle with a few drops of olive oil here and there, and repeat these alternate layers till the supply of fish is exhausted. Finally, pour over the whole a glass of wine vinegar, and let it stand for not less than two hours.

Marinade of Fish

Boiled fish
Onion
Pimento
Bayleaf
Cloves
Red pepper
Wine vinegar
Olive oil

These days beef, veal and lamb will be rarer—mostly cutlets, I fancy, *noisettes* and *tournedos* in their many beguiling varieties. Devilled meats, fish and vegetables will be popular, too. The larger joints will appear more often cold, *fricandeau* of veal or cold *daube* of beef or mutton, all supremely fine dishes and well worth the little extra trouble they demand.

Among the vegetables we have four newcomers, Globe Artichokes, Broad Beans, Runner Beans and Vegetable Marrow. Pulling the artichoke apart without getting your fingers abominably buttery is a game played in the highest circles, but we must try eating the *fonds* by themselves, whether served *à la parisienne* (that is browned in butter and accompanied by some small mushrooms cooked likewise and sprinkled with lemon and parsley), or *à la Clamart*, again, with peas. They also remind us of chicken *en casserole*, stuffed with liver, mushrooms and onion and cooked with thin sliced potatoes and artichoke bottoms. This is a tremendously good dish that never lacks acclaim.

Globe
Artichoke
Bottoms
à la
parisienne

à la Clamart

Broad Beans present a problem as knotty as any, that is, when once shelled, to peel or not to peel. Though I confess to a morbid attraction to the bitterish skin when moistened with melted butter, avaunt, I say, these lovely beans unpeeled and enslimed in parsley sauce! Let us rather peel them and eat a colourful purée of them when next we cook a gammon, or make a course of them alone 'cohered', as the cookery books say, with a sufficiency of thick fresh cream.

Broad Beans

Runner Beans or, more picturesquely, Scarlet Runners, like French Beans, can only be cooked in one way, to my thinking. And oh, always cooked whole. Nor must we attempt to dry them over the fire after they have been drained, but *sautez* them over a flame with a few small pieces of butter and some salt and pepper. A little chopped parsley may be added, if liked, but it must be very young and freshly gathered.

Runner Beans

Vegetable Marrow, again a sufferer from that unholy White Sauce which surely the worst of Bad Cooks invented to cloak her hideous misdeeds, is watery and insipid if improperly treated. If we are allowed to pick the tiny young ones, they are delicious boiled and served with butter. You do not even need to skin them. Fried their elder brothers can be, but they are better if cooked *à l'orientale*.

Vegetable Marrow and Lamb (à l'orientale)

Marrow
Cold lamb
Stock
Nutmeg
Grated cheese
Breadcrumbs

Cut them into slices, fairly thin, and soak them in cold salted water for half an hour. Mince some cold lamb and moisten it with a little stock, and season with nutmeg, salt and pepper. Fry the slices of marrow. Now in a buttered fireproof dish put a layer of the mince and another of the marrow. Sprinkle with grated cheese, then repeat the other layers, and so on till the dish is full, sprinkling at the last with grated cheese and breadcrumbs. This you cook for half an hour or so in a moderate oven till the top is brown, and delight your marrow-detesting friends by giving it to them for luncheon.

Peas with Bacon

Peas
Lettuce
Pickled pork or Bacon
Onions
Butter

We have been eating Peas for some time now, so it will do us no harm to be reminded how otherwise they can be cooked. An unusual way is to cook them in very little water with a piece of butter, the heart of a lettuce cut in four, two rashers of pickled pork or green bacon cut in small pieces, and half a dozen button onions and salt and pepper. Or you can use pork fat instead of butter. Before crying, Vandal! make the experiment yourself.

Cherry Pudding

Flour
Eggs
Milk
Sugar
Black cherries

It is time, too, to cook some cherries, those lovely black ones whose flesh is so sweet and melting. Jules Claretie, the famous French author, has given a recipe for a Cherry Pudding called *Clafoutis Limousin*. Put three tablespoonfuls of flour and a pinch of salt into a bowl and break and mix into it one by one three eggs. Add a pint and a half of milk by degrees, and three tablespoonfuls of castor sugar. Put about a pound and a half of black cherries into a fireproof dish, and pour this mixture over them. Bake it in the oven, and serve it with more sugar sprinkled over the top.

Cherries

Black cherries

Another way of serving Black Cherries is to stone a pound of them and stew them in sugar and water, gently so as to keep them whole. Let them get cold and add a couple of tablespoonfuls of Kirsch or Maraschino. In as many champagne glasses as you need place a macaroon, and on this pour your cherry compote to three-quarters of the way up the glass. A covering of stiffly whipped cream on top, and some chopped pistachio nuts on that.

Kirsch or
Maraschino
Macaroons
Whipped cream
Pistachio nuts

Currants I have left to the last, because I like them least. White ones have a pseudo-delicate flavour which just befits them for dessert. Black ones are tolerable once in a way in a pudding, when one is very hungry. The red ones, I admit, are an essential part of Summer Pudding which, I maintain, should be made with stale sponge cake instead of bread. Currants look very pretty at dessert, but they have unduly large pips, and their flavour is in general quite execrable. But stay! I do them an injustice, for I have forgotten red currant jelly, and the black-currant flavouring which makes some cough lozenges palatable!

*　　*　　*

There are days even in July when soups are welcome. Cauliflower Soup may well be one of them.

Cook a cauliflower in boiling salted water for twenty minutes, then cut it in half. Set half aside and keep it warm, and pass the other through a coarse sieve. Now chop a small onion and a stick of celery (in the summer use celery salt in the seasoning) and fry them for a few minutes in two ounces of butter with a bayleaf. Take out the bayleaf and stir in an ounce of flour. Add to this two pints of

Cauliflower
Soup

Cauliflower
Onion
Celery
Bayleaf
Flour
Butter
White stock
Milk

white stock, stirring well. Meanwhile boil a pint of milk and mix it with the cauliflower purée and then add it to the stock. Season to taste, strain, and put in the rest of the flower which you have broken into small pieces. Serve with *croûtons* of fried toast.

Eggs en
cocotte

Eggs *en cocotte* make a pleasant summer course, and are by no means unacceptable for breakfast. The little *cocottes*, like tiny earthenware saucepans, are familiar to us all. The simplest way is to butter the *cocotte*, break the egg into it, put a dot of butter on it and bake in a tin of boiling water for seven or eight minutes. Some cover them, some do not: it is a matter of taste. Eat the eggs out of the *cocotte*, or turn them out and serve on buttered toast.

Eggs en
cocotte à la
crème

These little dishes are susceptible of the same variations as eggs *sur le plat*. To cook them *à la crème*, you simply put into each *cocotte* a tablespoonful of boiling cream before breaking in the egg. A mixture of chopped bacon, mushrooms and onion makes a very savoury foundation for a first course at luncheon, or chopped chicken's liver, onion and bacon. To cook them plainly and pour a little hot tomato sauce over them is favoured by some, or a rich mushroom sauce could be used, and so on. But this is one of those dishes in the concoction of which your inventiveness can be exercised to your own delight and that of your friends.

Cold Eels with
White Wine
and Paprika

Eels
White wine
Paprika

I have mentioned certain ways of preparing Cold Eels. Here are one or two of them, suitable for a substantial *hors d'œuvre*.

This one could be prepared when you are making a *matelote*. Boil the eels in exactly the same way as for the *matelote*, save that you use white wine and

paprika seasoning. Let them get cold in the liquor.
Take them out and cut them into large fillets, remove the grease from the liquor and cover the
fillets with it.

This one would be amusing to make, if you can
get all the herbs, for you want two ounces of sorrel,
a quarter of an ounce of parsley, a few leaves of
tarragon, a little fresh pimpernel, two ounces of
tender nettle, a quarter of an ounce of savory, a
sprig of green thyme and a few sage leaves. Skin
two pounds of small eels, discarding the heads, and
cut them into pieces two inches long. Chop the
herbs and put with them the pieces of eel which
must now be well stiffened. Then add a pint of
white wine and a little salt and pepper. Cook for
ten minutes, then stir in four egg yolks and a few
drops of lemon juice. Serve very cold. You see, it is
quite easy to make—if you can get the herbs.

Cold Eels au Vert

Sorrel
Parsley
Tarragon
Pimpernel
Nettle
Savory
Thyme
Sage
Eels
White wine
Eggs
Lemon

So is the next. Stiffen the pieces of eels, cut as
before, in a little butter, moisten with a pint of beer,
season and cook for ten minutes. Add the same
chopped herbs as in the previous recipe, cook for
another ten minutes, and thicken with a little potato
flour. Serve this very cold also.

Cold Eels à la flamande

Eels
Butter
Beer
Herbs as before
Potato flour

Fillets of Sole *Victoria* must find a place in your
next dinner-party. Fold the fillets in two and cook
them in butter and the liquor from some mushrooms. Place the fillets in a circle on a dish and place
in the centre pieces of lobster and truffles which have
been tossed in butter. Cover the whole with
Béchamel sauce, sprinkle over the top grated Parmesan cheese, pour over a little melted butter and
put under the grill or in the oven till golden. Or the

Sole Victoria

Fillets of sole
Butter
Mushroom liquor
Lobster
Truffles
Béchamel sauce
Parmesan

fillets could, of course, be stuffed with the lobster. (The truffles could be omitted in an emergency.)

Devilled Crab

Crab
Béchamel sauce
Anchovy essence
Chutney
Chilli vinegar
Mustard
Cayenne
Breadcrumbs
Parsley

Devilled Crab is an excellent dish.

Flake the meat of a boiled crab and mix it with a sauce made of a quarter of a pint of white sauce, a dessertspoonful of anchovy essence, the same of chutney, a teaspoonful of chilli vinegar and the same of made mustard, seasoned with salt, pepper and cayenne. Put the mixture back into the shell, or into little *coquilles*, cover lightly with browned breadcrumbs, and bake in a moderate oven for about a quarter of an hour. Sprinkle with chopped parsley before serving very hot.

Lobster à la Crème

Lobster
Brandy
Butter
Paprika
or Cayenne
Eggs
Cream
Sherry or
Madeira

Lobster *à la crème* would be excellent for a late supper when the host's or hostess's prowess with the chafing dish might be on view. Cut the lobster in slices (a cooked one, of course), pour a liqueur-glassful of brandy over them, and set it alight. (This preliminary might be omitted, but if you are cooking it at the table, it is a pretty start.) Then cook the pieces for a few minutes in butter, seasoning them with salt, pepper, and paprika or cayenne. While they are cooking, beat up the yolks of two eggs with a little cream, and add a dash of Sherry or Madeira. Combine this with the lobster, and stir it slowly and carefully on the lowest possible heat till the sauce is thick. It must not boil on any account, and this is where the chafing dish comes in. But a gas ring with an asbestos mat over it might do just as well.

Lobster au gratin

Lobster
Mornay sauce

Lobster *au gratin* is another simple form of cooking this favourite shellfish.

The simplest way to do this is to warm up the pieces of a cooked lobster in Mornay sauce. Put them and the sauce back into the shells, sprinkle with grated Parmesan and brown under the grill. The sauce should be rather thick, and flavoured with a little cayenne or paprika pepper.

Parmesan
Cayenne or
Paprika

An original way of cooking shrimps and peas was recently shown to me. It was called Shrimps *à la chinoise.*

Shrimps
à la chinoise

Soak four and a half ounces of mushrooms (very young pink ones should be used, or those in a bottle) in water with a dash of vinegar for ten minutes, then cut them into small dice. Cut the same amount of lean bacon or ham into the same-sized dice, and brown them lightly in butter. Add half a pound of shelled peas, and cook them for half an hour, covering the pan with a soup-plate containing hot water. A spoonful or two of water may be added if the peas show signs of getting hard or dry. While this is cooking, fry half a pound of shelled shrimps in butter in a separate pan. They must not get brown or dry. In yet another pan now cook the mushrooms in butter to which a small chopped onion has been added. When they are done, add the bacon and peas and shrimps, cooking them all quickly together and shaking them for a few minutes so that their flavours are slightly blended. Season to taste and serve hot.

Shrimps
Mushrooms
Water
Vinegar
Bacon or Ham
Peas
Onion

A slightly different way of grilling kidneys is to split, core and skin them, pour melted butter over each, cover with breadcrumbs and grill for five minutes or so. They should be served on little rounds of mashed potato, with some *maître d'hôtel* butter on each.

Grilled
Kidneys
Kidneys
Butter
Breadcrumbs
Mashed potatoes
Maître d'Hôtel
butter

Veal Cutlets can be served with Apples in this way.

Veal Cutlets
with Apples

JULY

Veal
Butter
Parsley
Apples
Lemon
and possibly
Tomato sauce

Season some veal cutlets, pour some melted butter over them and grill them. When they are cooked, make a few incisions in each and cover them with a paste made of butter, chopped parsley, pepper and salt. Dish them round a purée of apples, which has been made by cooking a pound of apples in a little water with sugar and a few pieces of lemon rind and passing it through a sieve. Tomato sauce can be handed separately, if liked.

Sweetbread
and
Cucumber
Salad
Lettuces
Salad dressing
or Mayonnaise
Sweetbread
Cucumber

A cold salad of Sweetbreads and Cucumber is a happy idea.

Shred some lettuces and toss them in salad dressing or light mayonnaise. Lay them on a dish and place on them some slices of thinly sliced cooked sweetbread. Spread a mayonnaise over this and garnish with sliced cucumber.

Ham Loaves
Potatoes
Ham
Butter
Eggs
possibly
Nutmeg and
Parsley

Breakfasts or picnics are both equally well served by these little Ham Loaves. Cook and mash a pound of potatoes and mix them with a quarter of a pound of grated lean ham, an ounce of butter, two beaten eggs, salt and pepper. Grated nutmeg and chopped parsley can be added, either or both, if you care to do so. Mould the mixture into little loaves and fry them, or bake them in the oven, in the latter case gilding them with beaten egg. Serve hot for breakfast, cold for picnics. They are not too hammy in these cold-ham-and-salad days.

Stuffed
Chicken
en Cocotte
Chicken
Onions
Mushrooms
Chicken's liver

The advent of Globe Artichokes demands this stuffed chicken—a young one, please.

First make a stuffing by frying in butter for five minutes two or three small onions cut in slices. When they are getting brown, take them out and put in half a dozen sliced mushrooms. Cook these for a few minutes. Chop up the liver of the chicken (or two, if you can get another), and mix it with the mushrooms and onions. Stuff the chicken with this mixture (inside, not in the crop).

Cook, in a *cocotte* large enough to hold the chicken, a couple of rashers of bacon or pickled pork cut into cubes, with a piece of butter the size of an egg. When the bacon is cooked, take it out and brown the chicken in the butter, turning it on all sides. Now put back the bacon and add half a dozen potatoes cut in thin slices and some artichoke bottoms quartered. Cook all together without a lid for half an hour. Then take everything out of the *cocotte* except the gravy, pour in a small quantity good stock and white wine, and let it reduce a little. Season, put back the chicken and the other ingredients and serve as it is. No other vegetables are needed with this admirable dish. If you do not like the taste of wine, leave it out.

Bacon or Pickled pork
Potatoes
Artichoke bottoms
Stock
White wine

Chicken Maryland is a famous dish, but we are sometimes not quite sure of its composition.

Cut the chicken in pieces, season them, dip them in butter, roll in breadcrumbs and fry them in butter. They should be served with a rasher of grilled bacon between the pieces, and surrounded by small fried cakes of maize flour and fried slices of banana. A horseradish sauce enriched with cream is sometimes handed separately.

Chicken Maryland
Chicken
Butter
Breadcrumbs
Bacon
Maize flour
Banana possibly
Horseradish sauce and Cream

The aubergine has already been introduced, and I should like to make a few suggestions for making its better acquaintance. Fried slices of aubergine we have no doubt encountered, at any rate in a *Fritto Misto*, but this exotic-looking vegetable makes an extraordinarily good dish by itself, or accompanied

Aubergines à l'egyptienne
Aubergines
Onion
Oil
Cooked Mutton

Tomato
Parsley

by meat or a meaty stuffing. So here are one or two recipes, which I hope will be tried, for they deserve it.

Aubergines à l'égyptienne. Cut as many aubergines as you want in half lengthwise, and cook them gently in butter. When they are done, drain them and remove the pulp from their insides. Put the shells on the fireproof dish on which they are to be served. Now chop up the pulp, add to it a little chopped onion which you have fried in oil, and the same quantity of finely chopped lean cooked mutton as there is pulp. Fill the shells with this mixture, sprinkle with a very little oil and cook in the oven for a quarter of an hour. Just before serving the aubergines, garnish each half with a few rings of tomato lightly cooked in oil, and sprinkle chopped parsley over them.

Aubergines
à la provençale
Aubergines
Tomatoes
Oil
Garlic
Breadcrumbs
Tomato sauce

Aubergines à la provençale. Prepare them as above, but instead of adding onion and mutton to the pulp, add tomatoes tossed in oil and flavoured with a little garlic. Sprinkle the halves with browned breadcrumbs, brown in the oven and surround on serving with tomato sauce.

Fried
Aubergines

Fried Aubergines. Cut the aubergines into thin rounds. Season, dredge them with flour and fry in boiling oil. They must be drained and served at once, before they lose their crispness.

Aubergines
à la turque
Aubergines
Flour
Oil
Egg
Cheese
Batter or
Egg-and-
Breadcrumbs
Parsley

Aubergines *à la turque.* Cut each peeled aubergine into six slices lengthwise. Season, dredge with flour and fry these slices in oil. Then make a sandwich of two of them and put between them a firm preparation of egg yolk and finely grated cheese. Dip these sandwiches into batter, or egg-and-breadcrumb them, and fry them. Serve with fried parsley.

Cauliflower can be fried with great success. Boil it till it is nearly done, then take it out and dry it. Break the head into small flowerets and fry them in butter till they are golden brown. These flowerets can then, if desired, be treated *à la polonaise*, which has already been described for *petits poussins* and asparagus.

Fried Cauliflower à la polonaise

Another way is to marinate the boiled pieces for a quarter of an hour in a mixture of equal parts of water and vinegar, then to dip each piece in batter and fry in the usual way.

Cucumber can be fried, too, in the same way as the aubergine.

Fried Cucumber

Cook some inch-thick slices of peeled cucumber in boiling water slightly salted and flavoured with lemon juice, for ten minutes. Take them out, drain and dry them, flour them, egg-and-breadcrumb them and fry them. Grilled meat seems sometimes to demand this accompaniment.

Cucumber Lemon Flour Egg-and-Breadcrumbs

A simple stuffed-cucumber dish is this one. Split the peeled cucumbers lengthwise, and remove the seeds. Now stuff them with a mixture of fine breadcrumbs, grated onions, salt and cayenne or paprika pepper bound with melted butter. Bake them with a little good stock, with which they should occasionally be basted.

Stuffed Baked Cucumber
Cucumber Breadcrumbs Onions Cayenne or Paprika Butter Stock

To return for one minute to the aubergine, and to an Eastern dish, *Moussaká*.

Moussaká

Fry some aubergines cut lengthwise, and fry some small pieces of mutton strongly seasoned. Then arrange layers of the aubergine and mutton, moisten the mixture with stock and cook in the oven till the stock has disappeared. This is served with pilaff rice and a tomato sauce.

Another version adds tomatoes, shallots and parsley to the aubergines, omits the stock, and simply bakes in the oven for forty minutes.

Yet another advises the use of marrow instead of aubergine, which may be quite satisfactory, I should think, as a *pis-aller*.

And one I tasted not so long ago in a little Smyrnese restaurant in London was just made with slices of potatoes and minced mutton. But the flavour was authentic. An elastic dish, *Moussaká* (with the accent on the last syllable), and a most useful one, which we could well adapt to our convenience.

Flageolets

Flageolets are those pale green little haricot beans which come to us fresh in boxes. They can also be had by the pound dried, but are not nearly so good. They can be used simply boiled, and served with a little butter, or more delicately as a purée, known as *Purée Musard*. They are often used for thickening a purée of French beans, for which they are especially suited.

New Peas
Italian fashion

Lettuce
Peas
Butter
Egg
Cream
Sugar

This is an Italian way of cooking new peas.

Wash and tie up a lettuce and cook it with a quart of new peas in half a pint of salted water to which you have added a quarter of a pound of butter. As soon as the peas are done, take out the lettuce and keep it hot. Now beat up the yolk of an egg with a quarter of a pint of cream and add it, with salt, pepper and a good pinch of sugar, to the contents of the saucepan. Stir for two or three minutes, untie the lettuce, dish it and serve it with this mixture poured over it. And eat it as a separate course, please.

Strawberries
au vin

Now for the sweets of July! Two more strawberry suggestions, I think. First, if you are a little tired of strawberries and cream, try just sprinkling them with sugar and adding a tablespoonful of good red or white Bordeaux. Cream should *not* be taken with this.

Strawberries
Sugar
Red or White
Wine

The second is an easy strawberry cream. Pass half a pound of strawberries through a hair sieve, and add three ounces of castor sugar and the juice of half a lemon or orange. Melt half an ounce of gelatine in half a teacupful of milk and strain it on to the strawberry purée. Then whip half a pint of cream and fold it into it. Put into a mould and turn out when ready to serve. This should stand on ice for some time before being eaten, if it is possible.

Strawberry
Cream

Strawberries
Sugar
Lemon or
Orange
Gelatine
Milk
Cream

Here is a new savoury. Take some tips of boiled asparagus, and toss them in butter. Lay them on a piece of buttered toast, sprinkle them very lightly with grated Parmesan cheese, and brown quickly under the grill. If you wanted this dish rather richer, you could bind the tips with a little cream or the yolk of an egg before putting them on the toast. It is very good.

Asparagus
Tips with
Cheese

Asparagus
Parmesan
Buttered
toast
possibly
Cream or Egg

And here are two salads.

A slightly different taste in potato salad can be achieved by putting your cooked potatoes, thinly sliced and still lukewarm, into a salad bowl and sprinkling them with a good glass of white wine for each pound of potatoes. Season this with oil and vinegar when it is cold, and stir in carefully a little chopped chervil and parsley.

Potato Salad

Potatoes
White Wine
Oil
Vinegar
Chervil
Parsley

To make an orthodox cucumber salad, you should cut the peeled cucumber into thin slices, put them on a plate and sprinkle them with salt to bring out the water. After an hour drain the slices and

Cucumber
Salad

Cucumber
Vinegar

dress them with pepper and vinegar. But, barbarously, I shall always prefer my slices undressed and straight off the cucumber.

Home-made Pâté de Fois Gras

*Chickens' livers
or
Goose livers
Bacon
Thyme
Bayleaf
Brandy or Sherry
Cream
and possibly
Truffle*

This month's elegant extra is a tip for the picnic-goers and high-class tea-party givers. It is a home-made *Pâté de Foie Gras*. Do not conjure up visions of fatted geese breathing out their last on your lawn. This is a substitute, but in certain circumstances it might not be detected. You want a pound of chickens' livers or two goose livers, and a quarter of a pound of fat bacon. Cut up the latter into small pieces and fry them slowly in a frying-pan. Add the livers cut up small, a sprig of thyme and a bayleaf. Throw in a tablespoonful of brandy or sherry, cook for about ten minutes, take out the herbs and pound in a mortar. Then pass the mixture through a very fine sieve and mix it with a little cream, salt and pepper. If you can add some small pieces of truffle, do so now. Press down into little pots and, when it is quite cold, pour a little melted butter over each.

If you have the heart to deceive your friends, this is an excellent way of doing it, and if you are discovered, then the merit of making this excellent pâté is blushingly yours.

AUGUST

THE FOOD OF THE MONTH

Food which is in season all the year round is given in the table on page 19.

Note.—Newcomers are printed in italics.

FISH

Sea Fish

Haddock Hake
Herrings *Skate*
Whitebait

River Fish

Eels Salmon
Trout

Shell Fish

Crabs

MEAT

Lamb

POULTRY

Ducklings *Ducks*
Goslings Guinea-fowl

GAME

Blackcock *Capercailzie*
Grouse *Leveret*
Buck Venison
Wild Duck *Woodcock*

VEGETABLES

Globe Artichokes
Aubergines
Broad Beans
Cauliflower Green Peas
New Potatoes
Runner Beans Shallots
Vegetable Marrows
Watercress

FRUIT

Apricots Cherries
Currants Figs
Gooseberries
Greengages Melons
Mulberries *Loganberries*
Plums
Raspberries
Strawberries

EMPIRE IMPORTED FRESH FRUIT

Grape Fruit Limes
Naartjes Oranges

The following recipes are given during this month:

SALADS

ELEGANT EXTRA

While we are doubly thankful for holidays and the harvest to come, from clouds of dust and the spray of skimming yachts the spirit of August cookery arises, a little austerely, for in these languid days simplicity is the keynote of her mood. Appetites, she knows, are inclined to be fanciful, and smiling she presides over the hotel or club Cold Table, that pleasant engine for presenting a mass of food in the most seductive manner possible.

August gives thanks for the ingenuity of cooks and the harvested promise of our land

For these welcome ministrations Nature and man's invention offer her an ample choice on every side. All the fishes, save the mackerel, are here, with the addition of the Haddock, a dryish creature that requires much patient basting, but often admirable

Stuffed Haddock
*Streaky bacon
Onion*

Parsley
Eggs
Breadcrumbs
Butter
Bacon fat

if baked with the following stuffing. Fry crisply a couple of thin rashers of streaky bacon, and chop them up finely with three onions and a good handful of parsley. Mix them with two beaten eggs and enough breadcrumbs to stiffen well. A mixture of butter and bacon fat for the baking adds distinction to your Haddock stuffed in this way.

For meats, lamb and veal will be in the greater demand. Lamb cutlets *en chaud-froid* look amazingly appetising when set round a variegated pile of vegetable salad. Cold sweetbreads can be dressed in many attractive ways, and add dignity and substance to the salads they adorn. Pâtés, for summer luncheons or picnics, come into their own; and terrines, which are only pâtés without fawn and fragile crusts.

Cold
Duckling
aux
Mandarines

Duckling
Rice
Aspic jelly
Tangerines
Foie Gras

A cold duckling is always a pleasure, but if it is prepared *aux mandarines*, it provides a double delight. Roast it in the oven and let it cool in the liquor. When cold, lay it on a bed of rice and glaze it with aspic jelly. Surround it with tangerines hollowed and filled with a *mousse* of *foie gras*, and with little heaps of chopped aspic jelly to which, in the making, have been added the juices of the duck and the tangerines.

Mousseline forcemeat is easy enough to make, and often offers a happy solution of 'what shall we eat to-day?'—the gravest problem of the summer in this changeable climate of ours. All kinds of meat, poultry and fish yield deliciously to this treatment, and there are a hundred and one ways of varying the *mousselines'* appearance and flavour. *Mousselines* of chicken coated with Mornay sauce and served on a couch of spinach, *à la florentine*, are excellent, as they also are when coated with curry sauce and bedded on rice.

AUGUST

Goslings can now be had. Most of us will eat our first roasted and stuffed with sage and onions (and do not omit a little grated nutmeg), but the German fashion of braising him with a stuffing of apples and a garnish of more apples cored and filled with red-currant jelly should not be forgotten.

Roast Gosling. German fashion

*Goose
Apples
Red-currant
jelly*

And now, the triumph of the month, friend Grouse. None of us will forget the glorious Twelfth, for the noble promise it brings. But the true gourmand will look a little askance upon the air-borne firstlings on the dinner-tables of our expensive restaurants that night, preferring to wait a little till our bird is readier. September, rather, is the month in which to start eating him seriously, though perhaps August demands a grouse salad before the month is out, and we shall restrain with difficulty our impatience for cold grouse at the perfect breakfast.

In his wake come blackcock (a neglected bird), capercailzie (sometimes a little turpentiny), wild duck, the lissom leveret and the rarer woodcock: but these are also better for later eating. While the leverets are still young, a saddle cooked in the following way is supremely good. On the bottom of a dish long enough to contain it, lay the following vegetables: half a pound of minced carrots, the same of minced onions, two ounces of minced shallots, a crushed clove of garlic and a *bouquet* of thyme, parsley, bayleaf, and if possible rosemary. The saddle, which may be improved by fine larding (though, if it is very young, this is not necessary), is laid on this and set to cook. When it is nearly done, take out the vegetables and the *bouquet* and pour in a quarter of a pint of cream. Baste occasionally with this while the cooking is completed. At the last add

Roast Saddle of Leveret

*Leveret
Carrots
Onions
Shallots
Garlic
Bouquet garni
Cream
Lemon juice*

157

a squeeze of lemon juice, and serve the saddle with the cream sauce strained over it.

Potatoes Rissolées

Potatoes Butter Parsley or Chervil or Mint

Vegetables offer us nothing new in August. We lose asparagus, but we are rather tired of it by now. New potatoes, alas! are merely new in name only: the season of their infant waxiness is all too short. It is time to think of cooking them otherwise than by plainly boiling. For instance, *rissolées*, that is, half cooked in boiling salted water and then finished with butter in a casserole till they are golden and sprinkled on serving with chopped chervil or parsley or mint.

Potato Blanquette

Potatoes White sauce with Stock Mushrooms Egg

A *Blanquette* of them is often a novelty. While the potatoes are boiling (both for this and for the previous recipe they should be as small as possible), make a white sauce with a tablespoonful of butter, the same of flour and a breakfast-cupful of stock. Also have a few mushrooms cooking in butter. When the potatoes are done, add them with the mushrooms, salt and pepper to the sauce, and just before bringing to the table, stir in the beaten yolk of an egg.

Iced Polish Soup

Beetroot Cucumber Egg Parsley Chervil

By the way, when you have sated yourself with cucumber salads, you might try the cucumber soup already described. It can be made more interesting by the addition of spinach, and some chopped chervil, tarragon and parsley. I read somewhere the other day of an iced vegetable soup from Poland which sounded appropriate for August evenings. A beetroot cut in very small pieces was cooked in salted water, and while this was being done half a cucumber cut in thin slices was sprinkled with salt so that the water was exuded. The beetroot, cucumber, cucumber water, and the water in which the beetroot had been cooked were mixed together when cold, and to this were added slices of hard-boiled egg, chopped parsley and chervil, pepper and one well-beaten egg. It must be kept well iced, and at the very last moment pieces of ice were put into the individual cups in which this soup is served. I have not tried it yet, but I certainly shall do so.

Greengages, plums and mulberries are the new-comers among the fruit, all best eaten raw, and if possible warm off the wall or tree, as tomatoes should be eaten, too. Greengages make a good pie, and so do plums; and a really light plum pudding can attract many suet-lovers even in the height of summer. Mulberries are seldom come by, unless you have a fortunate friend with a tree in his garden. A luscious fruit, but rather messy. Loganberries are ripening, too. Their juice makes a particularly lovely jelly, both in colour and taste. It is too early yet for pears, I fancy, though ripe Williams will be on sale on all the south-coast town beaches. I doubt if they are natives, though. We might stew a few with some white or red wine, so much happier a dish than those forbidding dark red segments liberally be-strewn with cloves, which were so familiar in our childhood days.

A great month, August, fitted well for leisure and lovely food! Sad that, like the cuckoo to whom he bids farewell, 'go he must'.

*   *   *

Vegetable Marrow Soup, like Cucumber Soup, is light enough for summer eating.

Heat a quart of milk, and add to it two cupfuls of boiling water, two tablespoonfuls of minced onion,

Vegetable Marrow Soup

Milk
Water

Onion
Bayleaf
Celery
Marrow
Butter
Flour
Paprika
Cream

a bayleaf, quarter of a cupful of chopped celery (it will be easier to add celery salt to the flavouring later), and a good cupful of boiled marrow passed through a sieve. Make a thickening with three table-spoonfuls of butter and the same amount of flour with a little of the soup, stir this into the soup till it thickens, and season with salt, pepper and a little paprika. Cook for ten minutes together, strain and add a little cream. Or, if you serve it in separate cups, put a teaspoonful of whipped cream into each. (This is rather for decoration than anything else, for the soup tastes better if the cream is well blended into it.)

Cold Stuffed
Eggs

Cold Stuffed Eggs are useful for all meals this month, and their variety is legion. I remember that in my childhood they were invariably stuffed with anchovy, but though this is very good, it is not a patch on the many fascinating stuffings which have been and still can be devised. Escoffier has a pleasant little preamble on this subject, which should make the chests of all amateur cooks swell with expectant pride. 'The preparation of cold eggs', he says, 'is not limited by classical rules; it rests with the skill and artistic imagination of the operator, and, since fanci-fulness and originality are always closely allied to artistic imagination, it follows that the varieties evolved may be infinite.'

Although Escoffier includes under his heading of cold eggs, cold soft-boiled and even poached eggs, the stuffed hard-boiled egg is perhaps more suited to English palates. The principle to be observed is to mix up whatever flavouring is used with the yolk, moistening it if necessary with a little cream or even milk, or some sauce. You will be able at once to think of many savoury fillings, but here are some suggestions:

Finely chopped celery with cream, salt and pepper.

Mixed herbs and finely chopped onions, varied with chopped olives, pickled walnuts, pimentoes, and so on.

Foie gras. (Eggs Mimosa are eggs stuffed thus with *foie gras*, and covered with a sauce of one-third Béchamel and two-thirds mayonnaise sprinkled over with chopped yolks.)

Finely chopped lean ham. A dash of Worcester sauce can be added to this if liked.

Sardines, cod's roe, flaked haddock or kipper, tunny fish, tinned salmon, or various fish pastes, such as lobster, crab, etc.

Grated cheese.

Little pieces of very crisply fried bacon with a little chopped parsley.

Mushrooms.

A purée of asparagus.

Tomato purée highly seasoned, perhaps with a little grated cheese added.

These little eggs can be garnished in all manner of ways. They can be embedded in a salad, or placed on pieces of cold buttered toast, or on rings of cucumber or tomato. But in whatever form they appear, they are almost always certain to be welcome.

Grilled Salmon is possibly one of the finest manifestations of this lovely fish, and this is the time to delight in him before he goes. To serve him with Tomato Sauce is a change, and a fashion particularly suitable for Empire chilled salmon, which cannot yet claim the fine flavour of our river fish. This is an Italian dish.

Have the salmon cut in slices about an inch thick and put them in a buttered fireproof dish. Sprinkle them with salt, pepper, a little grated nutmeg, a teaspoonful of chopped parsley and two small

Marginal notes:

Eggs Mimosa

Salmon with
Tomato
Sauce

*Salmon
Nutmeg
Parsley
Shallots or
Onions
Claret or
Cider
Tomato sauce*

shallots (or onions) finely chopped. Dot with butter, and pour over a small glassful of claret or dry cider, if the latter is preferred. Bake for about a quarter of an hour, basting well. Keep the cutlets warm, and make a tomato sauce in which the liquid from the fish has been used, and pour this over the cutlets before serving.

Salmon au Citron

*Salmon
Lemons
Butter
Cream or
Milk*

Tinned fresh or smoked salmon can be made into an attractive dish in a hurry, if you have a few lemons in the house.

Pound the salmon well with butter, salt, pepper and the juice of a lemon, using enough butter to make the cream of the consistency you like. You will need to 'work' this paste for about a quarter of an hour, adding a little cream or creamy milk if it is too thick. Serve it in the scooped-out halves of lemons on a bed of salad. It makes an attractive and refreshing fish course, which might well be remembered as a stand-by for unexpected guests.

Smoked Haddock à la Tartare

*Haddock
Tartare sauce
Tomatoes
Hard-boiled eggs
Tarragon*

Another pleasant cold dish can be made by making a purée from the flesh of a cooked smoked haddock. Pour a thick Tartare sauce over it, and garnish with slices of tomatoes and hard-boiled eggs, and some chopped tarragon, if you can get it.

Sole en blanchailles

*Fillets of
sole
Flour or
Egg and
breadcrumbs*

An appetising way of having Fried Sole in the hot weather is to cut the fillets into very thin strips about three or four inches long. Either roll them in flour, or egg-and-breadcrumb them, and fry them. Serve while they are still crisp, with a sauce according to your fancy. Somehow the sole seems much lighter when treated in this amusing way.

A cold Crab *Soufflé* must certainly be embarked upon this month.

AUGUST

Boil a crab and remove all the flesh, setting aside one claw. Now mix the rest of the flesh, seasoned with salt and pepper, with a cupful of mayonnaise sauce and the same of liquid aspic jelly. Add four leaves of gelatine dissolved in a little warm water, and stir them into the mixture. Put half this mixture into a *soufflé* dish, then half the flesh from the claw you have kept back, then the rest of the mixture, and finally the rest of the claw. When cold, turn out on to a salad of lettuce and tomato.

Cold Crab Soufflé

Crab
Mayonnaise
Aspic jelly
Gelatine

Lobster *à la bordelaise* is another savoury manner of treating lobsters. Cut up two lobsters into fairly large pieces, keeping the shells, and boil these pieces for twenty-five minutes in some white wine seasoned with a clove of garlic, a *bouquet* of parsley, thyme and bayleaf, salt and pepper. The saucepan should be covered and the pieces stirred now and then. Take them out, dry them in a cloth and keep them warm. Brown two sliced onions in butter, stir in some flour and make a thick sauce with some of the liquor in which the lobsters were boiled. Cook for ten minutes, then add two tablespoonfuls of tomato sauce and some cayenne pepper. Warm up the pieces of lobster in this sauce and fill the shells with them. They can be browned under the grill, or not.

Lobster à la bordelaise

Lobsters
White wine
Garlic
Parsley
Thyme
Bayleaf
Onions
Tomato sauce
Cayenne

We have rather neglected the prawn, really because this finely flavoured fish is best eaten plainly boiled, though a very great deal is to be said for curried prawns, even when they come out of a tin. Prawn patties, however, would be delightful for an alfresco meal. They are worth the little extra trouble.

Put some boiled prawns, shelled, of course, into a wineglassful of sherry and a little lemon juice, and let them lie there for a little while. Make a flaky

Prawn Patties

Prawns
Sherry
Lemon
Pastry
Olives
Anchovy essence

163

pastry and line your patty pans with it. Into each of these put a few prawns and slices of olives, a little anchovy essence and a teaspoonful of the marinade in which the prawns have lain. Cover the patties with paste, and bake rather quickly till the pastry is nicely browned. If you cook it too slowly, the contents may become a little dry. You can, of course, serve these patties hot, but they are most excellent when eaten cold.

Lamb Cutlets en chaud-froid

Cooked lamb cutlets
Brown chaud-froid sauce
Aspic and possibly Truffle

I have mentioned Lamb Cutlets *en chaud-froid*. You should make them like this.

Cut and trim some cutlets from a neck of lamb which has been roasted, or better, braised. Dip each in a brown *chaud-froid* sauce (for which see the chapter on Sauces) when it is nearly cold, and sprinkle them with cold melted aspic. (A slice of truffle can be put on the meat part of each cutlet before the aspic is added.) Cut them out carefully when the aspic has set, and serve them round a mound of vegetable salad bound with a little mayonnaise thinned with thick cream.

Fricandeau

Veal
Stock
Carrots
Onions
Parsley
Thyme
Bayleaf
Garlic
Rind of bacon or Pickled pork

Fricandeau is another summer dish.

Get your butcher to cut a slice from a cushion of veal not more than an inch and a half thick. It must be cut with the grain of the meat. Beat it well, and lard it finely on the cut side. Now braise it with some good stock on a bed of sliced and fried carrots and onions (in the proportion of an ounce of each to a pound of meat), a *bouquet* of parsley, thyme and bayleaf, a clove of garlic and an ounce and a half of blanched rind of bacon or pickled pork. Cool very slowly till you can prick the meat deeply without any blood exuding. It must be cooked so long that it could be cut with a spoon,

nd indeed some connoisseurs demand that it should
never be cut with a knife on serving—which is a
little precious, I think. Anyhow, when it is cooked
to your liking, dish it very carefully lest it break,
clear and strain the braising liquor, pour it over the
ricandeau and let it get cold. The meat may also be
glazed, if a smarter appearance is desired, but the
liquor will set to a thick jelly, which can be adorned
with little heaps of cold cooked vegetables, such as
peas, beans, carrots and so on.

An unusual Ham dish hails from Canada. Boil
some Patna rice and drain it well. To this add the
same weight of cooked ham finely chopped, and
season well with salt, black pepper and cayenne.
Mix well together and serve with a salad of lettuce.

Mousselines and *mousses* are both made in the same
way, the former merely being little *mousses* which
re served separately to each guest, instead of his
helping himself from the larger *mousse*. We will consider *Mousselines* of Chicken, though they can be
made in the same way from other meats, poultry,
game, fish and shellfish.

Cut into cubes a pound of cooked chicken meat,
from which you have removed the skin and the
tendons. Season it with an ounce of salt, a little
pepper and nutmeg, and finely pound it to a paste.
When the paste is ready, add gradually the whites
of two eggs, working it well the while. Now rub it
through a fine sieve, put it into a basin, stir a little
more with a wooden spoon, and stir in very gradually a pint of thick fresh cream. To cook the *mousselines*, put them in the oven in *dariole*-moulds and
cook *au bain-marie*, or they can be poached and well
drained. They can be eaten hot with various sauces

*Ham and
Rice*

**Mousselines
of Chicken**

*Chicken
Nutmeg
Eggs
Cream*

and garnishes, or cold coated with aspic. Ham and lobster *mousses* occur to us at once. Here are a few variations on the chicken theme.

Poach them and coat them with a Mornay sauce. Serve them with a heap of asparagus tips or new peas tossed in butter.

Poach them and coat them with Indienne sauce. Serve rice with these.

Poach them and coat with a *suprême* sauce flavoured with paprika. Surround with a pilaff of rice in which you have mixed some chopped tomatoes cooked in butter.

Poach them and serve them either coated with *suprême* sauce and on a bed of macaroni with tomato sauce, or coated with the same sauce on a bed of spinach. In both cases sprinkle with grated Parmesan cheese and glaze quickly in the oven.

Salmi of Hazel Hen

Hazel hen
Onion
Carrot
Shallots
Flour
Tomato
Red wine
Stock
Mushrooms

Hazel Hen is a most delicate bird when it has been newly shot, but cold storage does not exactly improve it for roasting. This *Salmi*, which is also suitable for other game birds, offers a good way of presenting Hazel Hen at the table.

Roast the birds, but not too much: the flesh should still be pink inside. Carve them up into pieces, removing the skin and the ends of the legs which are inclined to be bitter. Keep these pieces warm and make the following sauce:

Pound up the carcases and fry them till brown in a little butter with some chopped onion and carrot and one or two shallots. When they are ready, add a little flour, and let that brown, too. Now add a quartered tomato, a glassful of red wine, and enough stock (game stock if possible) to make the sauce the right consistency, which at the end should

e thick and creamy. Cook this slowly for an hour.
Towards the end of that time cook in butter some
small fresh mushrooms, adding the trimmings to
the sauce, which you must strain when it is finished
and pour over the pieces of bird. Warm the whole
thing thoroughly, and serve garnished with the
mushrooms.

You can add some triangular sippets of fried
bread, if you like: and if you are afraid of the pieces
of bird getting dry while they are keeping warm,
you can add to them a little melted meat glaze and
a drop or two of burnt brandy. This *salmi* can also
be made from cold cooked birds, but it will not
then be as good.

We have noticed one or two forms of hot cucumber. The following is rather interesting:

Cut a large peeled cucumber into small squares, a
layer of which you must put in the bottom of a
buttered fireproof dish. Season these pieces with
grated onion and lemon juice. Cover with breadcrumbs and dabs of butter, seasoning with plenty of
paprika and some celery salt. Repeat these layers till
the dish is full, ending up with crumbs and butter.
Cover and bake for an hour till brown. A *sauce
piquante* might well accompany this curious dish.

Cucumber au paprika

*Cucumber
Onion
Lemon
Breadcrumbs
Paprika
Celery salt*

It has been said that the ability to prepare one
good dish of *petits pois à la française* is the hall-mark
of a good cook. Here is one method of preparing
this famous dish.

Put the peas, which should be as nearly the same
size as possible, into a casserole with some butter,
a little salt, the hearts of two small lettuces, a *bouquet*
of parsley, mint and cloves and a half-dozen small
button onions, or spring onions. Cook over a slow

New Peas (petits pois à la française)

*Peas
Lettuces
Parsley
Mint
Cloves
Onions*

Bread-and-butter
Flour

fire, stirring carefully from time to time. Do not add
any water. When they are nearly cooked, put in a
small piece of bread-and-butter which has been
dipped with flour. Serve them with the onion and
the lettuce, if you like, but without the other in
gredients—and see if you are hall-marked.

Stuffed
Pimentoes

Pimentoes
Onions
Stock
Tomato purée
Rice

Here is a way of stuffing pimentoes, those beau
tiful red or green vegetables which are now adorn
ing the more enterprising greengrocers' windows
As a matter of fact, with a little care, the tinned one
could be stuffed very well, so long as they are wel
dried, but the fresh ones are far better.

This stuffing is enough for six large ones, green
or red. Cut off the tops of the pimentoes and scoop
out very carefully, so as not to break the skins, the
seeds and the pith. Chop up two onions with the
tops of the pimentoes, and cook them in butter til
soft and nicely browned. To this add salt, pepper
a teacupful of stock and two tablespoonfuls of
tomato purée (tinned will do, if you haven't time
to make fresh). Add to this a teacupful of rice
which has been half cooked in boiling water and
well drained, and finish cooking it in the sauce. Add
a little butter, and strain the sauce, keeping aside
the liquid which comes from it. Stuff the pimentoes
with the mixture, and cook them in the oven in a
buttered fireproof dish with the liquid poured over
for fifteen minutes. They must be kept fairly moist
by basting, so you may need to have a little extra
stock ready. You may find it advisable to fry the
pimentoes a little (but very lightly) before stuffing
them, but it is enough usually simply to bake them.

Tomatoes can also be stuffed and baked in the
same way, but they will not take quite so long.

No repertory of potato dishes would be complete without *maître d'hôtel* potatoes. This is one way of cooking them.

Maître d'hôtel
Potatoes

New Potatoes
Béchamel sauce
Lemon
Butter

Boil some new potatoes and cut them into slices while hot. Then put them into a saucepan with a little white sauce, a squeeze of lemon juice, pepper, salt and a little butter. Stir all together and serve hot.

Another way is to boil the potatoes in their skins, peel them, cut them into slices, shake them well in a saucepan with a nice piece of butter, and just before serving sprinkle in, while shaking, some finely chopped parsley.

Two seasonable sweets are Cream of Rice and Rice *à l'impératrice*.

Cream of
Rice

Rice puddings can be very delicious, especially if, as my experience of the softest and creamiest rice pudding I have ever tasted tells me, it has been put in the oven last thing at night and left there till morning. But modern conditions and gas cookers often make such cooking impossible; so many will prefer a Cream of Rice which makes a splendid border for fruits of various kinds. It is very simple to make, though it takes a little time. All you have to do is to put a couple of tablespoonfuls of Carolina rice into a pint of cold milk. Add half a dozen lumps of sugar and a vanilla pod (which can be taken out at the end, dried, and used again). Cook *very* slowly in a double saucepan till the milk is absorbed. This will be a good three hours. Let it grow cold and then mix in a little fresh cream.

A really splendid refinement of this is called Rice *à l'impératrice*.

Rice à
l'impératrice

Rice

Cook the rice as for a cream and while it is cooking cut up some preserved fruits, a little angelica

Preserved fruits Angelica Mixed peel Glacé pineapple Kirsch

and mixed peel, and some glacé pineapple into very small pieces and soak them in a little Kirsch. Add them to the rice when it is ready, and stir in also a liqueur-glassful of Kirsch. Pour into a buttered mould and, when it is cold, turn it out. If you like you can add a super-refinement in the form of a layer of red-currant jelly at the bottom of the mould, or serve the cream with a red-currant syrup.

Half-Mourning Salad

Truffles Potatoes Mustard sauce Cream

Here are one or two salads which may be useful for August meals.

If some special dish has meant the opening of a bottle of truffles and there are a few over, a salad with the picturesque name of *Demi-deuil* (Half-mourning) can be made by mixing some *julienne* strips of truffles with a *julienne* of cold waxy potatoes, and seasoning with a mustard sauce to which a little cream has been added.

Apple and Cucumber Salad

Another rather unusual salad is made from apples and cucumber. Season equal parts of sliced cucumbers and apples with salt, pepper and a sprinkling of lemon juice. Bind them with a little whipped cream, and serve quickly.

Pimento and Cucumber Salad

Pimentoes and Cucumber also make a good salad. Cut the pimentoes, fresh or tinned, into pieces and the cucumbers into cubes, or you can mince both finely (letting the cucumbers lie in a bowl sprinkled with salt for half an hour or so to exude their moisture), drain them, mix them, and season with pepper, oil and vinegar, and add some chopped chervil at the last or, failing that, some parsley.

Cucumber, Lobster and Asparagus Salad

A more elaborate cucumber salad is composed of dice of lobster, cucumber, asparagus heads, and truffles, seasoned with a mayonnaise sauce coloured with a purée of lobster coral.

Beef Salad is a meal in itself.

Cut some boiled or roast beef into little cubes. Mix it with some sliced tomatoes, cold boiled potatoes, chopped parsley and spring onions. You can also add chopped gherkins, celery, herring fillets or anchovies, and it is always pleasant to have one of these fishes in it. Dress it with a simple dressing of oil, vinegar, salt and pepper.

Tomatoes are served in America as follows, as a salad or an *hors d'œuvre*. Cut them in thin rounds and marinate them for twenty minutes in oil, salt, pepper and a dash of vinegar. Arrange them on a dish with rings of very finely cut raw onion.

Tomatoes can be served cold and stuffed in a variety of attractive ways. A new flavour, for instance, can be found by filling them with tunny fish mixed with tomato juice and finely chopped herbs.

These are one or two other suggestions for stuffing them—when cold, of course:

Yolks of hard-boiled eggs mixed with mayonnaise and sprinkled with chopped parsley.

Russian salad, or any mixed cooked vegetables such as beans, peas, potatoes, carrots, moistened with mayonnaise.

Tunny Fish mixed with the above. (Tunny Fish, which can be bought in tins, makes a very delightful *hors d'œuvre* when served as it is.)

Tinned salmon mixed with a little mayonnaise.

Strips of cheese, tongue, apples and celery mixed with mayonnaise.

Quite an uncommon ice can be made, by the way, from tomatoes. Make a purée of raw tomatoes and strain it through a hair sieve. Flavour it with a little salt and pepper, and freeze slightly to make an ice of it.

Beef Salad
Beef
Tomatoes
Potatoes
Parsley
Spring onions
and possibly
Gherkins
Celery
Herring fillets
or Anchovies

Tomatoes à
l'américaine
Tomatoes
Oil
Vinegar
Onion

Cold Stuffed
Tomatoes

Tunny Fish

Tomato Ice

SEPTEMBER

THE FOOD OF THE MONTH

Food which is in season all the year round is given in the table on page 19.

Note.—Newcomers are printed in italics.

FISH

Sea Fish

Bloaters	*Conger Eel*
Dab	Haddock
Herrings	*Ling*
Skate	Whitebait

River Fish

Eels	Salmon
	Trout

Shell Fish

Crabs	*Oysters*

MEAT

Lamb	*Pork*

POULTRY

Ducks	*Geese*
Goslings	Turkeys

GAME

Blackcock
Capercailzie

Grouse	*Hares*
Leverets	*Partridges*
Ptarmigan	*Quails*
	Rabbits

Buck Venison
Wild Duck Woodcock

VEGETABLES

Globe Artichokes
Aubergine
Brussels Sprouts
Red Cabbage Cauliflower
Green Peas
New Potatoes
Runner Beans
Shallots
Vegetable Marrows
Watercress

FRUIT

Apricots
Blackberries

Currants	*Damsons*
Figs	Gooseberries
Grapes	Greengages

Loganberries

Melons	*Nectarines*
Peaches	*Pears*
Plums	*Pumpkins*
Quinces	Raspberries

Strawberries

EMPIRE IMPORTED FRESH FRUIT

Apples	Grape Fruit
Limes	Naartjes
Oranges	Pears
	Plums

The following recipes are given during this month:

SALADS

ELEGANT EXTRAS

Of all the gastronomic months of the year, I think September holds out to us the greatest riches. She is the month *par excellence* for a superabundance of fish; the principal game birds are all with us save the pheasant, and he is not far off. Her radiant cornucopia of fruit is overflowing.

And ah! oysters are here again. I see visions of ecstatic epicures astride at oyster-bars with the glistening bivalves poised at expectant lips. Nothing but a hiatus, thus . . . . expressive of indescribable delight, can give them adequate welcome. Let us give praise in a silence of gustatory anticipation!

The lucky September holiday-maker at the seaside

With September's store another cycle, and the more serious business of eating, begins, and cook welcomes a wider choice of fare

can now indulge in fried dabs for breakfast, and the
village fish-seller will yield up two excellent boiling
fish, ling and conger. The latter always reminds me
of an old Cornish fisherman who on his rounds used
to complain to me: 'Cunger! Mid as well put a
helephant in yer basket as cunger, 'cep' for Tredavoe
folk: they'll eat un!' Tredavoe being the next village,
and a long way for him to walk with his basket. It
is, however, quite wrongly despised, and makes an
excellent soup. Skate is another neglected fish, possibly owing to its repulsive appearance. But Skate
au beurre noir is really delicious. Have the skate
filleted, and boil the fillets in water to which you
have added a sliced onion and a little vinegar. Cook
it, drain it well and serve it with sprigs of fried
parsley and black butter. The latter is made by frying a handful of parsley sprigs in butter till they are
crisp and brown. Continue browning the butter
without burning it, and just before serving pour it
into two tablespoonfuls of boiling lemon juice. You
can add a dash of vinegar, if you like. But it should
convert you to Skate.

Hake goes off the list this month, and we must
not forget to have a parting dish or two of trout
and salmon before they, too, leave us. Trout *au bleu*
is suitable for a September repast. Make a *court-
bouillon* of half a pint of white wine and the same of
water, an onion and a carrot cut up, a *bouquet* of
parsley stalks, thyme and bayleaf, and some salt. If
you wish, you can add a leek cut up, a little celery
and tarragon. Simmer this for an hour, for the last
twelve minutes of which you have added a dozen
peppercorns. Strain, and in this boil the trout carefully. Some people prefer melted butter with this,
others a *mousseline* or *hollandaise* sauce.

Skate au beurre noir
Skate
Onion
Vinegar
Parsley
Butter
Lemon

Black Butter
Butter
Lemon juice
possibly
Vinegar

Trout au bleu
Trout
White wine
Onion
Carrot
Bouquet garni

SEPTEMBER

Pork is now added to our meaty fare, and Turkeys to our poultry. It always seems a strange thing that turkey should be relegated so severely to Christmas time, for he is a delicate bird when young. Suppose we celebrate his return by having him roasted with a stuffing of chestnuts cooked in *consommé* or stock, and made into a purée with some very finely chopped pork, in proportion of half and half. And as Brussels sprouts are also with us once more, we can equally celebrate them by eating them with him.

There will never be an end to the discussion as to which is the best of the game birds. I plump for grouse, but partridge runs him very close, and now is the time to see. Never better, I believe, than roasted is this little grey darling of the fields, but to serve him with cream is a fetish of some. Cook him in butter in an earthenware saucepan with a smallish onion cut in quarters. When he is three-quarters cooked pour over him a cupful of cream into which you have mixed a few drops of lemon juice. Baste him with the cream while the cooking finishes and serve up in the saucepan.

We can now eat our grouse more happily. The quail comes to us from the south, and the snowy ptarmigan from the north. In the mushroomy fields the rabbits are gambolling in innocence of their impending sacrifice; and, by the way, those mushrooms will make a very savoury accompaniment to their tender flesh.

If we cannot have broad beans with our pork, we can certainly have Red Cabbage. I doubt if pickled red cabbage should even be permitted with Lancashire Hot Pot, though it is the Northern custom, and it is possible that those who abhor this un-

Margin notes:

Turkey
Roasted

*Turkey
Chestnuts
Pork
Consommé or
Stock*

Partridge
à la crème

*Partridge
Butter
Onion
Cream
Lemon*

Hot Red
Cabbage

*Red cabbage
Onion
Cayenne*

Nutmeg
Butter
Sugar
Vinegar

pleasant pickle have never tasted the cabbage treated in any other manner. This recipe may be a revelation to many, especially with boiled knuckle of pork. Slice a red cabbage very finely, and soak it in water for about half an hour; then put the pieces in a saucepan with an ounce of butter, a tablespoonful of chopped onion, a saltspoonful of salt, cayenne pepper and grated nutmeg. Cook with the lid on till the cabbage is tender (about an hour), then add a dessertspoonful of sugar and a tablespoonful of vinegar. Cook all together for another five minutes.

Blackberry
Fool

Temptation to many lurks in a blackberry pie, hot or cold, *pace* the dentist; but give me a simple Blackberry Fool, concocted by straining a pound of blackberries cooked in just enough water to cover them and properly sweetened into a pint of not-too-whipped cream. So many of us can never forgive blackberries—and raspberries, too—for their venomous little pips! Damson cheese seems to be the best use for these rather harsh little plums. It is quite pleasant with some meats, in place of red-cur-

Pork Cutlets
with
Compote of
Quinces

rant jelly. Quinces are also for jam-making, but there is a fashion of serving fried egg-and-breadcrumbed pork chops or cutlets with a compote of this unusual fruit. This would seem to have distinct possibilities.

Pumpkin
Soup

Pumpkin
Butter
Milk
Sugar
French roll

I suppose the monstrous but ornamental pumpkin should be considered a fruit, rather than a vegetable, though it is on the border-line. Pumpkin Pie, so beloved of our Transatlantic cousins, I have never sampled. Pumpkin Soup is for the adventurous who have a pumpkin thrust upon them. Cut a ripe pumpkin into small pieces, boil them for seven minutes in just enough slightly salted water to cover them, and pass them through a wire sieve. Now melt a couple of ounces of butter in a saucepan, add the purée of pumpkin and leave it on a low flame for ten minutes or so. Into this stir a pint of boiling milk, a pinch of sugar, salt and pepper. Simmer gently for a few minutes, and serve. You can put a few thin slices of stale French roll in the bottom of the tureen, if you like this habit.

For fruit, pears are now supremely edible. Their names read like a catalogue of vintage wines: Winter Nelis, Jargonelle, Fondant des Bois, Bon Chrétien, Comice, l'Epine d'Eté. And peaches! These, too, like plums and greengages, must be eaten off the wall, if you want them at their best. The Gargantuan superfluity of this lovely fruit in our overseas orchards must make them only fit for their final beatification in peach-fed Ham. The best imported peach I ever tasted came from Italy, and it had all the mellow sunshine in it. But nectarines—blest appropriate name!—must be eaten quickly from the tree and still almost warm from the caressing sun. And who will say that they do not bear off the palm?

* * *

I doubt if my old Cornish fisherman, or rather his wife, would have taken as much trouble over a Soup of Conger as I am about to advise; but to marinate fish would be nothing unusual for them. Ling, I think it is, that is usually marinated in Cornish villages; but I know little more about it than my memory of the great fillets of fish hanging up to dry on the clothes-lines—made fast with the clothes-pegs, too.

Conger Soup

Conger eel
Onions
Parsley
Thyme
Bayleaf
Garlic
Potatoes
Tomatoes

Well, for this soup cut a fresh conger eel into pieces about four inches long, put these in an earthenware jar and cover them with coarse rock salt. Leave the jar in a cool place for two days in warm weather, or four days in cold. This is a very important preliminary.

When you want to make the soup, wash as many pieces of fish as you will need, wipe them, and fry them for a few minutes with a good piece of butter in the saucepan in which the soup is to be made. Take the fish out and fry till brown two or three onions cut up very finely. Add as much water as is required, a *bouquet* of parsley, thyme and bayleaf, a little garlic, one or two potatoes and an equal quantity of tomatoes, some salt and plenty of pepper. Boil up, cook till the potatoes are done, add the pieces of fish and cook for another hour or so. Just before serving take out the *bouquet*, and press the fish well with a fork, so as to distribute its flavour throughout the soup. Stir a little, and serve the soup quite roughly, as it is.

Eggs sur le plat

Eggs *sur le plat* are another form of egg-cooking which rightly has many adherents in preference to the other forms.

They can be cooked either in separate little dishes or several on a dish. Just cover the bottom of the dish with melted butter, break the egg or eggs into it, put a dash of melted butter over the yolks with a sprinkle of salt, and cook in the oven till they are lightly done. About half an ounce of butter should be used for each egg.

These eggs can be varied in as many ways as the

SEPTEMBER

soft-boiled eggs and eggs *en cocotte*, indeed perhaps more, as there is a little more room for the garnishings.

Some like Eggs in brown or black butter. They can be prepared either by cooking the eggs *sur le plat* as usual, and then covering them with a little brown butter to which a few drops of vinegar have been added; or by cooking half an ounce of butter till it is almost black. Break the eggs into this, season them and cook them. Slip them on to a dish, rinse the pan with a few drops of vinegar, and pour it with the butter over the eggs.

Eggs with Black or Brown Butter

All sorts of extras can be added to make eggs *sur le plat* a more substantial dish. For instance, little grilled sausages with tomato sauce; sliced chicken's liver cooked in butter with a little chopped onion and paprika; a purée of spinach with a Mornay sauce (Eggs *à la florentine*); a Mornay sauce alone; small tomatoes, plain or stuffed; grilled kidney; various mincemeat and so on, besides the suggestions made for eggs *en cocotte*.

Herrings baked with rice and tomatoes is a dish that might be tried for luncheon one day.

Herrings with Tomatoes

*Herrings
Tomatoes
Rice
Lemon or
Vinegar*

Take some herring fillets and cut them in half crosswise. Also skin some tomatoes, and have ready some boiled and well-drained rice. Now put a layer of the fillets in a buttered fireproof dish, and over them a layer of tomato slices. Sprinkle over this salt and pepper and a little lemon juice, or vinegar if you prefer it. Cover with the rest of the fillets, on these spread the rice and, lastly, the remaining tomato slices. Dot with butter, and bake for about three-quarters of an hour in a moderate oven.

Red Mullet can be grilled *en papillote* or not. Have

Grilled Red
Mullet, I

*Red Mullet
Oil
Lemon
Parsley*

the mullets cleaned without removing the liver. Then cook them in either of these two ways.

Wipe them and make a few gashes on either side. Season them with salt and pepper, sprinkle them with a little oil and a few drops of lemon juice and lay them on a bed of a few slices of lemon and some parsley stalks. Let them marinate thus for a couple of hours, turning them every now and then. When this process is over, grill the fish carefully, sprinkling them the while with the marinade. It will take about twenty minutes. When serving, hand separately a little half-melted *maître d'hôtel* butter.

Grilled Red
Mullet, II

*Red Mullet
Oil
Lemon
Parsley
Pork fat*

The second way of grilling them is to marinate them as before, but when you come to grill them, wrap each in a *papillote* of strong oiled paper together with a little of the marinade, a little parsley and a few tiny bits of raw pork fat, and grill them very gently. Serve them as they are, in the paper bags.

Mussels
(Moules
marinières)

*Mussels
Onion
Garlic
Parsley
White wine*

One last recipe for Mussels, the renowned *Moules marinières.*

Scrape and clean the mussels well. Then chop together very finely an onion, a clove of garlic and some parsley, and put this with the mussels, salt, pepper, a small piece of butter and a glassful of white wine into a saucepan. Cook quickly for about a quarter of an hour, and your mussels are ready.

Mrs. Virginia Woolf has a little rhapsody on Beef *en daube* in *To the Lighthouse.* Readers of that fine novel may like to know a way of cooking such a noble dish. Others may well profit by the recipe. It is another such dish as the *fricandeau* of veal which we have already discussed, and, of course, can be eaten

SEPTEMBER

hot or cold. The only quarrel which some epicures would have had with Mrs. Woolf's Mr. Bankes would arise from his eating it with a knife and fork, when, they would maintain, only a spoon should be used. (I believe, as a matter of fact, that this dish is called in some parts of France *Bœuf à cuiller*.)

This is the Provençal fashion, according to Escoffier, and I give his recipe as it stands.

Cut four pounds of shoulder or cushion of beef into cubes weighing about four ounces each. Lard each piece with a strip of bacon two inches long by half an inch wide, and put them into a bowl with salt, pepper, a very little spice, five or six table-spoonfuls of vinegar, and a glass of red wine. Leave them to marinate for two or three hours, and toss the pieces from time to time so that each may be well saturated. Heat six ounces of grated bacon in an earthenware stewpan, and brown in the fat twelve small onions, fifteen carrots cut in the shape of olives, two sticks of celery cut into pieces of the same size as the carrots, and four cloves of garlic. Add the pieces of meat, which should have been properly dried; fry the whole for a further seven or eight minutes and moisten with the marinade and two more glasses of red wine. Now add half a pound of fresh bacon rind, blanched and cut into square pieces of two-thirds inch side, a *bouquet* of parsley, thyme and bayleaf and a small piece of dry lemon rind. Set to boil, completely close the stewpan, and leave to cook in a moderate oven for six or seven hours. When about to serve remove the *bouquet*, clear all grease from the gravy and serve in the pan in which it was cooked.

If you want to eat it, or the remains, cold, take out the pieces with a fork and place them in a

Beef en daube
à la
provençale

Beef
Bacon
Spice
Vinegar
Red wine
Onions
Carrots
Celery
Garlic
Parsley
Thyme
Bayleaf
Lemon

terrine with the untouched pieces of carrot, onion and bacon. Strain the gravy over them, and leave to cool. Then turn them out on to a dish and garnish with chopped aspic jelly.

Fricassée of Sausages with Carrots

Carrots
Sausages
Parsley
Onions
Lemon
White wine

A *Fricassée* of sausages with carrots rings the changes on our sausage dishes.

Parboil some carrots, cut them in slices and finish cooking them in butter. Put them in a fireproof dish with some grilled sausages (the Parisian kind), a little chopped parsley, some fat from the sausages, a small pat of butter, a few small onions chopped and fried, a drop or two of lemon juice and a glassful of dry white wine. Cook all together for a few minutes longer and serve in the same dish.

Dutch Omelette

Flour
Milk
Eggs
Parmesan
Peas
or Asparagus tips
Béchamel sauce
Ham

A Dutch Omelette, which is more like a pancake, is a fairly substantial dish.

Have ready some batter made of milk, flour, the yolks of four eggs and the whites well whisked and folded in. Make a fairly thick and fairly light pancake and slip it from the pan on to the dish on which it is to be served. Keep it warm and sprinkle on it plenty of grated Parmesan cheese. Then make another pancake, lay it on top of the first and sprinkle it with finely chopped ham. One more pancake on top of this, and then adorn the whole edifice with green peas or asparagus tips, fresh or tinned according to the season. Finally, pour a creamy white sauce over the whole, and serve very hot.

Liver with Olives and Apples

Onion

An unusual way of cooking liver is the following.

Chop up an onion and fry it in butter till brown. Stone and chop a few olives, and fry them with the bacon, and some salt and pepper, for a few minutes longer. Meanwhile in another pan, fry in butter or bacon fat some pieces of liver which have been rolled in flour and seasoning. Dish the pieces of liver, sprinkle the onion and olives over them, and surround them with some well-drained quarters of cored and peeled apples which have been poached in water till tender.

Olives
Bacon
Liver
Apples

A chicken cooked *en cocotte* is sometimes welcome as a relief from roast or boiled fowl.

Brown the chicken in butter in a covered *cocotte*, till it is half cooked. Then add some small dice of pickled pork which are well fried, a dozen button onions partly cooked in butter, and twice the number of pieces of potato the size and shape of olives. Finish cooking all together. A little veal gravy can be added at the last, if you have any.

Chicken
en cocotte

Chicken
Pickled pork
Onions
Potato
Veal gravy

A Russian *Blanquette* of Chicken can be made from a roast fowl, as follows. Cut as many slices as are wanted from the breast of a roasted fowl (or other pieces of the fowl would do) and remove the skin. Make a Béchamel sauce, and when cooked cut up a small cucumber into thinnish slices. Stew these in the sauce and, when they are done, pour it all over the chicken, adding a few tablespoonfuls of cream at the last moment.

Russian
Blanquette
of Chicken

Chicken
Béchamel sauce
Cucumber
Cream

We have been eating our grouse for some time now, but before the winter comes we should have a Grouse Salad. To make the sauce for this mix two finely minced shallots with half a dozen teaspoonfuls of tarragon and chervil mixed together, five dessertspoonfuls of castor sugar, the yolks of two eggs, five saltspoonfuls of salt and pepper mixed, and a pinch of cayenne. Stir these ingredients into

Grouse Salad

Grouse
Shallots
Tarragon
Chervil
Sugar
Eggs
Cayenne
Oil

Chilli Vinegar
Cream
Beetroot
Anchovy
Hard-boiled egg

a dozen tablespoonfuls of salad oil and six dessert-spoonfuls of chilli vinegar, and finally a quarter of a pint of whipped cream. Pour this sauce over the pieces of cold grouse, which you have surrounded with beetroot and pieces of hard-boiled egg and anchovy.

Rabbit
en casserole

Rabbit
Onions
Mushrooms

The simplest and one of the most pleasant ways of cooking a rabbit—a young one is best—is to cut him up into pieces and to put them with a good piece of butter in a casserole. Fry them till golden brown, add a few button onions, salt and pepper, put the lid on, and cook gently till the rabbit is done. Take off the cover now and then and let the water which has formed inside run into the casserole, to help with the gravy. A few mushrooms tossed in butter might be added with advantage towards the end of the cooking.

Mushrooms
à la crème

Mushrooms
Butter
Parsley
Thyme
Bayleaf
Eggs
Cream
Nutmeg

And mushrooms remind me that they are very good when cooked *à la crème*. Peel the mushrooms and remove their stalks, and if they are at all large cut them into quarters. Melt a couple of ounces of butter in a stewpan, and add the mushrooms and a *bouquet* of parsley, thyme and bayleaf. Toss them on a good flame till the mushrooms are done, then take out the *bouquet* and pour off all but a very little butter. Beat up the yolks of two eggs with a gill of cream, add them to the mushrooms and stir until the mixture is cooked. Season with a little salt, pepper and grated nutmeg, and serve very hot.

Potato
Soufflé

Potato purée
Cream
Eggs

Potato *Soufflé* is a very different thing from Potatoes *soufflées*.

For the first you want about a pint of potato purée enriched with a little cream, well-whipped and fairly stiff. To this add the yolks of three eggs and their whites stiffly whisked. Season it well and cook in a buttered *soufflé* dish for about a quarter of an hour in a moderate oven.

Two things must be observed about Potatoes *soufflées*. They must be very carefully cooked (for they are difficult to do), and they must be served immediately.

Peel the potatoes and cut them into slices about the thickness of a penny. Wash the pieces and dry them well and fry them in fat which must be hot, but not boiling. When they come to the top, take them out and bring the fat to the boil. Then put the pieces back, about half a dozen at a time (not more, or the temperature of the fat will be reduced), stir the fat and the potatoes should puff up. Only experience can teach you how to accomplish this dish, the success of which is better assured if you use soapy potatoes rather than floury ones.

Potatoes
soufflées

Potatoes
Frying fat

While pumpkins are in, we should try our hand at a Pumpkin Pie. Here are two ways of making it.

Pare and halve a ripe pumpkin, take out the seeds and cut it into thick slices. Stew it gently with a little water till it is tender, then pass it through a fine sieve to make a purée. Take half a pint of this, add two ounces of sugar, the yolks of two eggs, three-quarters of a pint of milk, a little mace or nutmeg, and at the last the two egg whites stiffly frothed. Put this mixture into a pie-dish, cover with short-crust paste, as for an ordinary pie, and bake in a quick oven.

Pumpkin Pie,
I

Pumpkin
Eggs
Milk
Nutmeg
Pastry

This is a simpler method. Pare, halve and cut the pumpkin into thin slices, removing the seeds. Put the slices into a pie-dish, seasoning each layer with

Pumpkin Pie,
II

Pumpkin

*Allspice
Pastry*

sugar and a little allspice. Cover with paste and bake as before.

These pies can both be served hot or cold.

Pears or
Peaches à la
Condé

Pears and peaches can each be used in the following ways, *à la Condé* and *à la Cardinal*.

*Pears or Peaches
Vanilla pod
Rice
Apricot
syrup
Kirsch*

For the first, poach the pears or peaches in sugared water to which you have added a vanilla pod, let them get cold and dish them on a border of cream of rice, covering them with apricot syrup flavoured with Kirsch.

Pears or
Peaches
à la Cardinal

For the second, poach the fruit as before, dish them when they are cold, and cover them with a very sweet raspberry purée flavoured with Kirsch and sprinkled with splintered fresh almonds.

*Pears or Peaches
Vanilla pod
Raspberry purée
Kirsch
Almonds*

Egg and
Cheese
Toast

Egg and Cheese Toast is a new savoury to many.

Rub the yolks of two hard-boiled eggs through a sieve, mix them with an ounce of butter and two ounces of grated cheese, and add salt and pepper and a little made mustard. Spread this mixture on squares of buttered toast pretty thickly, and brown them in a sharp oven.

*Hard-boiled eggs
Cheese
Mustard*

Macaroni
Cheese
(Swiss
fashion)

The Swiss manner of making a Macaroni Cheese is preferred by many.

Cook the macaroni in salted boiling water for ten minutes, then drain it. Now in a buttered fireproof dish put a layer of macaroni, sprinkle it well with grated cheese, and so on, ending with cheese. Cover this with breadcrumbs, dot with butter and cook in the oven till golden.

*Macaroni
Cheese
Breadcrumbs*

Endive and
Orange Salad

And here are four more salads.

Endive and Orange combine very well. Wash some endives (the long white kind), removing all the discoloured leaves, and cut them in half length-

*Endives
Oranges*

wise. Peel an orange or two and cut the rind into very thin strips. Boil these in water for a few minutes, and let them get cold. Arrange the endives in a dish and pour over them a sauce made of mustard, cream, salt, pepper and a little cayenne— the proportions to your taste's discretion. Sprinkle the orange strips over all.

Mustard
Cream
Cayenne

A Spanish salad can be made as follows. Peel and quarter some small tomatoes and cut some pimentoes (tinned ones are perhaps best for this) into very thin strips. Mix these with plainly cooked rice which has been allowed to grow cold, and add a little crushed garlic, and onion and parsley finely chopped. Season with oil and vinegar.

Spanish Salad
Tomatoes
Pimentoes
Rice
Garlic
Onion
Parsley
Oil
Vinegar

An Alsatian Salad affords a good way of using up various 'scraps'. Cut some cold boiled waxy potatoes into small pieces, and mix them with any or all of the following (with any additions or omissions you feel like); chopped cold chicken, small pieces of cooked beef, ham or bacon, anchovies or herrings in oil cut up small, beetroot, gherkins, and so on. Season with oil, vinegar, salt and pepper. This should be done about an hour before serving, so that the salad absorbs some of the dressing. Mix again at the last and sprinkle with chopped parsley and onion, if you like it.

Alsatian Salad
Potatoes
Chicken
Beef
Ham or Bacon
Anchovies or
Herrings
Beetroot
Gherkins
Oil
Vinegar
Parsley
Onion

Peaches and Plums can easily be pickled at home, and provide a very delightful adjunct to our dishes of cold meat. And Empire fruit is cheap enough to help us here.
Dip the peaches in boiling water for a moment, and then rub their skins off. Halve them and take out the stones, and stick two cloves into each half.

Pickled
Peaches

Peaches
Cloves
Brown sugar
Cinnamon
Vinegar

Pickled
Plums

Plums
Brown sugar
Cinnamon
Vinegar

Make a syrup of two pounds of brown sugar, an ounce stick of cinnamon and a pint of vinegar by boiling for twenty minutes, and cook the peaches in it, a few at a time, till they are soft. Let them get cold, and bottle them.

Plums can be pickled in the same way, halving and stoning them, but omit the cloves.

*   *   *

A NOTE ON HOT *HORS D'ŒUVRES*

The coming of winter evenings will give the enterprising hostess an opportunity of offering hot *hors d'œuvres*.

They are not commonly met with in England, and they are really our old friend, the Savoury, at the beginning instead of at the end of the meal. Savouries are not generally eaten in France, and it is the lighter kinds that can be served as *hors d'œuvres*. For instance, anchovies could be sent to the table *au gratin*, that is, covered with breadcrumbs and melted butter and browned in the oven; or as *allumettes*, each fillet lying on a couch of anchovy butter on a little strip of puff pastry and the whole baked in the oven; or they could be served simply hot on toast. Indeed, the *canapé*, or savoury on toast, the varieties of which are innumerable, is an excellent form of this kind of *hors d'œuvre*. You can surmount your fingers of toast with smoked cod's roe, with scrambled egg sprinkled with cheese or criss-crossed with thin strips of anchovy, or with a purée of smoked haddock. This latter can also be sprinkled with grated cheese, or garnished with an oyster or two cooked in a little Worcester sauce, or surmounted by a small grilled mushroom, or even a slice of tomatoes. Purées of this kind can be made from kippers, bloaters or even fresh salmon.

Of meat and vegetable mixtures for *canapés* there is no end, and amusing and succulent combinations offer endless scope for the ambitious amateur *hors d'œuvrier*. Chopped tongue or ham, with parsley and mushrooms, bound with the yolk of an egg; asparagus tips sprinkled with grated cheese and grilled a golden brown; chickens' livers and mushrooms and a taste of minced onion; a little chopped kidney; grilled mushrooms or tomatoes, and so on.

Bacon can come to our aid, too, so long as the rashers are streaky and of the thinnest cut, and it is crisply cooked. Roll them round oysters, chickens' livers, stuffings made from various forcemeats or potted meats, or tomatoes and mushrooms bound together with the yolk of an egg and a few fine breadcrumbs; the little rolls fried crisply or well baked before they grace their dainty pieces of toast. Eggs can be hard boiled, cut in half and filled with various mixtures combined with the yolk, and served hot with or without a sauce made to suit the filling. Tomatoes can also be hollowed out and stuffed a different way. You can also make tiny balls of any cooked mincemeat, yolk of egg and breadcrumbs and fry them in batter.

Pastry offers us cheese fingers and those delicious little *bouchées*, each like a miniature *vol-au-vent*, which can be served hot with countless different fillings of fish, shellfish, vegetables or meat. They can, of course, be bought, empty, from any good pastrycook; and this reminds me how much cheaper it should be to provide hot *hors d'œuvres* than cold

ones. Besides, any that were left over could be
warmed up and eaten just as pleasantly for luncheon
or as a savoury the next day, and one would not be
faced with the rather dismal aftermath of cold *hors
d'œuvres* which always look so bedraggled after their
first appearance.

But it must be remembered that the whole art in
presenting *hors d'œuvres*, whether hot or cold, depends on two things. First, they must be made as
attractive as possible, and, second, they must be
chosen carefully with an eye for the meal that
follows them. In the first case, they must be made
to supply a bright and pleasant opening to the meal
both to the eye and palate. In the second, while
hinting at the gastronomic delights that are to come,
they should never make the mistake of forestalling
them, and must therefore be selected in such a way
that the same sort of dish will not come after them.
That is to say, if you have salmon in the *hors
d'œuvre*, you should not have salmon in the fish
course; if *bouchées* as an *hors d'œuvre*, then never *vol-au-
vent* to follow. Such a planning of the meal is really
elementary, yet it is surprising how many ignore it.
Yet it should make the choice of the dishes and the
hors d'œuvres a labour not only of love, but of
fascinating interest.

OCTOBER

THE FOOD OF THE MONTH

Food which is in season all the year round is given in the table on page 19.

Note.—Newcomers are printed in italics.

FISH

Sea Fish

Bloaters	Conger Eel
Dabs	*Gurnet*
Haddock	Herrings
Ling	Skate
	Smelts

River Fish

Eels

Shell Fish

Crabs	Oysters

MEAT

Pork

POULTRY

Ducks	Geese
Goslings	Turkeys

GAME

Blackcock
Capercailzie

Grouse	Hares
Leverets	Partridges
Pheasants	*Plovers*
Ptarmigan	Quails
Rabbits	*Snipe*
	Teal
	Doe Venison
Widgeon	Wild Duck
	Woodcock

VEGETABLES

Globe Artichokes

Aubergines	*Broccoli*
	Brussels Sprouts
Red Cabbage	Cauliflower
Celeriac	*Horseradish*
	Parsnips
	Runner Beans
	Shallots
	Spanish Onions
	Watercress

FRUIT

Apricots
Blackberries

Damsons	Grapes
Medlars	Melons
Nectarines	Peaches
Pears	Plums
Pumpkins	Quinces

EMPIRE IMPORTED FRESH FRUIT

Apples	Grape Fruit
Limes	Oranges
Naartjes	Peaches
Pears	Plums

195

The following recipes are given during this month:

SAVOURY DISHES

SALADS

The holiday season is over, and at last we have more time for our culinary contemplations, and those who from pleasure or necessity cook for themselves will find the longer evenings leading them to the stove rather than to the open window.

The season of soups is upon us. Let us venture upon a few new ones. *Minestrone,* for instance, so beloved of Italians, and indeed of nearly all who have once tasted this national masterpiece. For this soup you will want some veal or chicken stock, and in it you must boil any vegetables that are at hand: potatoes, carrots, turnips, all cut in small slices, some shredded cabbage, a few onions sliced and lightly fried, chopped parsley, little pieces of lean bacon, a clove of garlic if you like it (but this should not remain in the soup for more than a

October woods and coverts complete the catalogue of game

Minestrone

White stock Any uncooked vegetables Parsley Bacon Macaroni or Spaghetti Cheese

199

quarter of an hour). Do not stint the vegetables, as there should be plenty, and introduce them into the stock in the order of their cooking, that is to say, put in first those that take the longest time to cook, so that all are finished together. About twenty minutes before serving, throw in some inch-long pieces of macaroni or spaghetti. Grated cheese sprinkled on each helping at the table is a *sine qua non*.

In October smelts, *éperlans*, which I am told are called sparlings in some parts of Scotland, come to us again, and are considered by some to be the most delicate of sea fish, having when fresh the smell of cucumbers, it is said, and according to others the perfume of violets. A very delicious morsel, in any case, whether baked or fried, and in my opinion a good exchange for whitebait, which we shall eat no more till the New Year. All the other fish remain, except salmon and trout, whose absence we have already anticipated by a few lingeringly savoured 'last appearances'.

Lamb is now grown up, and in the maturer form of mutton is approaching its best season. A saddle is unfortunately reserved for a larger concourse of diners than the ordinary home musters; but we must have a dinner-party, or visit as soon as may be one of those restaurants where this magnificent joint is a feature. A boiled leg of pork, with its essential concomitant Pease Pudding—but O, no parsnips!—is certainly to be recommended now that the weather is favourable to heartier eating.

Pheasant
à la crème

Normandy
Pheasant

With the advent of pheasant, plover, snipe and teal, game is now in full display. By the way, an infallible sign of the age of pheasant or partridge lies in the extremity of the last large wing-feather. If i is pointed, the bird is young, but if rounded this is an indication of age. Pheasant can be worthily cooked *à la crème* in the same manner as partridge, which I described last month. To cook him in the Normandy fashion will appeal to many. Fry him well in butter till he is nicely browned, and meanwhile toss in butter half a dozen peeled, cored and finely chopped apples. Put the pheasant in a casserole on a layer of apple, putting the rest round him, and sprinkle over the bird three or four tablespoonfuls of cream. Cover the casserole and cook in the oven for about half an hour. Serve in the same dish. Teal, widgeon and plover are usually roasted, but they make an excellent *salmi*, so long as the skin, which is inclined to be bitter, is discarded. Doe venison, so much more tender and delicate in flavour, is also an addition to the variety which our October table commands.

Pheasant
Butter
Apples
Cream

We must bemoan the disappearance of peas, and with them new potatoes and vegetable marrows. Broccoli and celeriac are the newcomers, the former so much more definite in taste than the cauliflower, the latter giving us an admirable salad if cut in fine *julienne* strips and seasoned either with a mayonnaise sauce to which an extra quantity of mustard has been added, or with a mustard sauce diluted with cream. Parsnips, those revolting roots, we shall rightly ignore, but Spanish onions we shall hail against those inclement days when a braised one, in spite of its social consequences, will be just the thing. These onions lend themselves to a variety of stuffings, for instance the following: Fry lightly a teaspoonful of minced onion in a tablespoonful of oil and butter mixed. Add to this four tablespoonfuls of chopped mushrooms (the washed parings and stalks will be even better than the heads), and stir it over the

Celeriac Salad

Stuffed
Spanish
Onions

Onion
Butter
Oil
Mushrooms
Nutmeg
Parsley
and perhaps
Sausagemeat

flame till the moisture from the mushrooms has disappeared. Then season with salt, pepper, grated nutmeg and a coffeespoonful of finely chopped parsley. Parboil the onions, scoop out the insides, and chop up the flesh you have taken out with an equal quantity of the mixture just described. Finish their cooking by braising. You can elaborate this by adding some sausagemeat to the stuffing mixture, and serve with a tomato or brown sauce. You can also stuff them with spinach, with a risotto, with potato combined with their flesh, or with semolina cooked in stock and flavoured with grated Parmesan cheese. Turnips can also be presented stuffed with this last mixture.

Stuffed Turnips

To our native fruit we must begin to say *au revoir* and at once to figs, currants, gooseberries, green-gages, raspberries and strawberries, though these latter have been for long in their decline. Medlars will appear at our dessert, somehow always reminiscent of autumn evenings and nuts and wine. Apples make good puddings, and to bake them on slices of fried bread with a liberal anointment of marmalade makes a very fine dish indeed. I am told that they can even make tapioca palatable. Here is the way for whoever cares to try it. Boil three tablespoonful of large tapioca very slowly in a pint of milk flavoured with lemon peel for three or four hours and while this is finishing stew in syrup half a dozen apples, peeled, cored and cut in not-too-small pieces. Put half the tapioca in the fireproof dish and on it half the apples. Repeat this, spread plenty of apricot jam over the top, and bake in the oven for twenty minutes. Serve hot, of course, and I have an idea that marmalade might advantageously be substituted for the jam.

Apples baked with Marmalade

Apples and Tapioca

Apples
Tapioca
Milk
Lemon
Apricot jam
or Marmalade

October is a cheesy month, Stilton and Wensley-dale, that finer cousin, making their prime appearance. Cheese dishes, too, are welcome for luncheon. *Gnocchi alla Romana* are a savoury form of semolina. Sprinkle a third of a pound of semolina into a pint of boiling milk, and after adding salt, pepper and grated nutmeg, simmer gently for twenty minutes. Now, off the fire stir in the yolk of an egg, and spread out the mixture to cool in a layer about half an inch thick. When cold, cut it into small rounds or squares, put these pieces in a buttered fireproof dish, sprinkle them liberally with a mixture of grated Gruyère and Parmesan cheese and a little melted butter, and bake in a moderate oven for twenty minutes. Some people like to add a thick tomato sauce to this exquisite dish.

Gnocchi alla Romana

Semolina
Milk
Egg
Butter
Cheese
Nutmeg

* * *

A Creole Soup made from Rabbit shall be our next experiment.

Cut two young rabbits into small pieces and put them in a stewpan with two quarts of cold water. Chop up an onion and add it to the water, with a blade of mace and a bayleaf. Bring to the boil and simmer for two hours. Now add salt, pepper and cayenne pepper, and half a cupful of rice. Simmer for another hour, and when serving add a couple of tablespoonfuls of sherry.

Creole Rabbit Soup

Rabbits
Water
Onion
Mace
Bayleaf
Cayenne
Rice
Sherry

The weather will now allow us to eat our stuffed eggs hot, an unfamiliar way, perhaps. Ingenuity can again be exercised in the composition of the stuffings and in the choice of sauce to accompany it. Here are one or two variations.

Hot Stuffed Eggs, I

Hard-boiled eggs
Onion
Anchovy
Parsley
Breadcrumbs
possibly
Tomato sauce

Having halved the eggs, chop up the yolks with an onion, a few fillets of anchovy, a little parsley and some pepper. Cook this in butter for a few minutes, then stuff the whites with it, put them in a fireproof dish, sprinkle with breadcrumbs, a dab of butter on each and brown under the grill or in the oven. You could serve a tomato sauce with this if you cared to.

Hot Stuffed Eggs, II

Hard-boiled eggs
Mushrooms
Lemon
Béchamel sauce

Cook a few mushrooms in butter for about ten minutes. Season them with salt, pepper and a squeeze of lemon juice and chop them up with the egg yolks, binding with a little Béchamel sauce. Stuff the eggs with this, put them in a fireproof dish with some of the sauce poured round them, and brown slowly in the oven.

Plaice cooked with Mushrooms

Plaice
White sauce
Mushrooms
Thyme
Basil
Parsley
Allspice

Plaice can be cooked with Mushrooms, too.

Scald the fish, make scores in the top and rub into them a tablespoonful of butter with a little salt and pepper. Let it bake in the oven in a buttered fireproof dish for a quarter of an hour, and meanwhile make a sauce of butter, flour and fish stock. Add to this sauce a few mushrooms, a sprig of thyme and basil (or a very little of these herbs dried), two sprays of parsley and six allspice all chopped very finely. Cook for five minutes longer, pour it over the fish, return the dish to the oven and cook for another quarter of an hour.

Baked Smelts

Smelts
Anchovy essence
Lemon
White wine

Smelts are once more in season. Fried smelts are the best, I think, but much can be said for them when they are baked like this:

Arrange them in a dish (in which you will serve them) in which you have put a little butter, a drop or two of anchovy essence, the juice of a lemon and a glass of white wine. Sprinkle them with salt, cayenne pepper and a little ground mace, cover them with breadcrumbs, dot them with butter and bake till they are brown.

Cayenne
Ground mace
Breadcrumbs

By the dainty-fingered, smelts can be stuffed with chopped fried onions, mushrooms, oysters and parsley bound together with a thick white sauce. But not for me.

Baked Stuffed Smelts

Here is a good way of cooking Sole.

Have a sole filleted, and put the trimmings into a saucepan with a small carrot sliced, half a stick of celery also sliced, a teaspoonful of parsley, a clove, a *bouquet* of parsley, thyme and bayleaf, and enough water to cover them. Bring to the boil, simmer for an hour and strain. Fry a sliced onion in butter till golden, add half an ounce of flour and stir in half a pint of the fish liquor till it thickens. Leave this on the side of the fire, having seasoned it, and cook the sole by tying the fillets into knots, putting them into a buttered fireproof dish with a little butter, covering them with buttered paper and baking them in the oven for a quarter of an hour. When they are done, add their liquor and a dessertspoonful of chopped parsley to the sauce, which you will pour over the fillets.

Sole
Lyonnaise

Fillets of sole
Carrot
Celery
Parsley
Clove
Thyme
Bayleaf
Water
Onion

South African dishes do not, I find, differ very much from what we are used to at home; but this one does a little.

Soak a thick slice of bread in half a pint of milk, and mash well with a fork so that there are no lumps. Now fry two medium-sized onions, sliced, in an ounce of butter, and when they are cooked add to them the baked bread, two tablespoonfuls of

South African Meat Custard

Bread
Milk
Onions
Curry powder
Sugar
Almonds

Lemon
Egg
Beef

curry powder, a dessertspoonful of sugar, half a dozen almonds finely chopped, a tablespoonful of lemon juice, an egg, half a teaspoonful of salt and two pounds of lean beef finely chopped. Mix all this well together, and put into a buttered pie-dish. Beat up another egg with the milk left from soaking the bread (it must be made up to a good quarter of a pint), season with salt and pepper, and pour over the mixture in the pie-dish. Bake till the custard is set. Cooked or uncooked beef can be used, but the latter will take about twice as long to cook.

Roast Leg of
Mutton à la
provençale

Mutton
Anchovy
Garlic

This is the Provençal way of cooking a leg of lamb or mutton, and very well worth trying. Lard a leg of lamb or mutton with about a dozen inch-long fillets of anchovy, and put a little piece of garlic near the bone. Roast it in the usual way, basting it well. Keep it hot and clear the gravy of grease.

For the Sauce

Onions
Shallots
Anchovy
Gherkins
Tomato purée

The leg should be served with the following sauce. Cook two small onions and two shallots, both finely chopped, in a little butter; sprinkle in a little flour and cook a short while longer. Chop up two anchovy fillets and two or three gherkins, and add these with a small spoonful of tomato purée and the gravy from the meat to the onions and flour. Stir well, cook a little longer, season well and serve with the joint.

Frikadeller, I

Raw Veal or
Pork
Butter
Breadcrumbs
Eggs
Nutmeg
Onion
Stock

Frikadeller are a kind of meat rissole, made either of veal or, in the Danish fashion, of pork. They can be made of raw or cooked meat. (These quantities are for ten of them.)

With raw meat. Mix a pound of very finely chopped meat with two-thirds of a pound of butter. Add five ounces of well-pressed breadcrumbs soaked in stock, two beaten eggs, half an ounce of salt, a little pepper and grated nutmeg, and two ounces of chopped onion cooked in butter without browning. Mix well together, divide into ten portions, which you can roll into balls or shape into round flat cakes, brown them on both sides in butter and finish cooking them in the oven.

With cooked meat. Put into a bowl large pinches of salt and pepper, and a little grated nutmeg. Add the contents of three medium-sized baked potatoes, three ounces of chopped onion fried in butter without browning, a pound of finely chopped cooked veal (using the fat and lean), one egg and a tablespoonful of chopped parsley. Mix, divide and cook as in the recipe already given.

Frikadeller, II

Cooked veal
Nutmeg
Potatoes
Onion
Egg
Parsley

These *frikadeller* can be served with a purée of vegetables, and with a *sauce piquante*. In Denmark they are accompanied by a brown or tomato sauce, and sometimes even with beetroot or cucumber or some pickled peaches.

A Casserole of Tripe is an inexpensive and excellent dish.

Casserole of Tripe

Tripe
Oil
Vinegar
Shallot or Onion
Mushrooms
Flour
Tomato purée
Breadcrumbs

Cut some well-cooked tripe into strips and marinate it for a little in oil and vinegar in equal parts. While it is soaking, fry a minced shallot, or onion, golden in butter, and add half a pound of mushrooms cut in thin slices. Cook for ten minutes or so, then remove them. Stir into the butter an ounce of flour, add two cupfuls of fresh tomato purée and stir till the sauce thickens. Butter a casserole, and put into it a layer of half the tripe, then a third of the sauce, all the mushrooms, more sauce and half a cupful of breadcrumbs. On this spread the remainder of the tripe, then the rest of the sauce and more breadcrumbs. Dot with butter, and bake in the oven for about twenty minutes, when the top should be an elegant brown.

Veal Pudding

Veal
Ham, Bacon or
Pickled Pork
Suet paste

Veal makes an uncommon pudding.

Cut two pounds of lean veal into smallish pieces, keeping the bones and trimmings aside. Also cut up half a pound of ham, bacon or pickled pork into thin strips. Line a basin with suet paste, put in the meat, with here and there the pieces of bacon, seasoning well with salt and pepper, and proceed as when cooking a beefsteak-and-kidney pudding. Cook it for three hours, during which time you will have made a good gravy from the trimmings, to be served with the pudding.

Chicken Croquettes with Oysters

Cooked Chicken
White sauce
Celery salt
Cayenne
Lemon
Onion
Oysters
Egg and
Breadcrumbs

Another American dish of chicken is made in this way.

Moisten a cupful of cold finely chopped chicken with a little white sauce, seasoning it with salt, celery salt, cayenne pepper, lemon juice and onion juice. Parboil as many large oysters as you will need, drain them and cover them with the chicken mixture. Roll these little croquettes in breadcrumbs, then in egg, and then in more breadcrumbs, and fry in deep fat.

The sauce for this dish should be made with butter and flour and some of the liquor in which the oysters were cooked, and enriched with cream.

Partridges with Cabbage

Cabbage
Partridges

Partridges with Cabbage is a remarkable way of using old birds. Allow half a partridge to each person.

Cut a good-sized savoy into four, and boil it. While it is cooking put the partridges into a casserole with some butter, a carrot, an onion, a piece of fat bacon, salt and pepper, and brown on a moderate fire. Then add a tablespoonful of flour, mix in and pour on a cupful of stock. Also put in a *bouquet* of parsley, thyme and bayleaf. Cover and boil for twenty minutes. After this is done put in the cabbage and a few chipolata sausages. They must all be just covered with the sauce. Add a little more stock if necessary. Cover the casserole again and cook very gently till the birds are done, which will be a good hour at least. Then put the cabbage on a dish and place on top the partridges, untrussed and halved, and the sausages.

Carrot
Onion
Bacon
Stock
Parsley
Thyme
Bayleaf
Sausages

Quails are so delicious when plainly roasted that any adornment seems a pity. Still, it is worth remembering that they can be served *à la Normande* in the same way as the pheasant mentioned a few pages previously. They can also be cooked in a casserole with butter and anointed with a gravy made from the butter in which they have cooked, a little rich game stock and a few drops of brandy. The principal thing is not to be afraid of cooking these little birds at home. So long as precautions are taken against their getting too dry, they will be just as delicious and certainly cheaper than in a restaurant. Just as delicious, did I say? Much more delicious, I should have said; for according to the proverb at the beginning of this book, '*On ne mange bien que chez soi*'.

Quails

Brussels sprouts can often be made more attractive if, after they have been cooked, they are put back into the pan with a good piece of butter, some pepper and a little grated nutmeg; then put into a fireproof dish, sprinkled with some grated cheese, perhaps moistened with a little cream, which is browned quickly under the grill.

Brussels
Sprouts
au gratin
Brussels sprouts
Butter
Nutmeg
Cheese
possibly
Cream

O'Brien
Potatoes

*Potatoes
Tinned
pimentoes
Spanish onion
Parsley*

Tinned pimentoes can be combined with potatoes in this manner. Peel some potatoes and scoop them out into little balls with a special scoop till you have a quart of balls. Throw them into cold water as you scoop them out, and, when they are all done, drain them well and fry till tender in deep fat. Fry two thin slices of Spanish onion in butter till golden, take them out, and in the same fat fry lightly two large tinned pimentoes cut in small pieces. Add the fried potatoes, mix together, sprinkle with a tablespoonful of chopped parsley, and serve very hot.

Devilled
Potatoes

*Potatoes
Butter
Mustard
Vinegar
Cayenne
Eggs*

Boil a dozen or so small waxy potatoes. To devil them, put two good tablespoonfuls of butter which have been combined with a teaspoonful of made mustard into a deep frying-pan, add a tablespoonful of vinegar, a little salt and a pinch of cayenne. Cook this mixture for three or four minutes, shaking the pan well; put in the warm potatoes, add the yolks of two eggs well beaten up and serve practically at once.

Potato Cake

*Potatoes
Bacon or
Onion*

Everyone knows the old way of cooking up cold mashed potatoes by frying a cake of them in the frying-pan under a plate. But many forget that this dish is far nicer if it is made with freshly boiled and mashed potatoes, which can be mixed with tiny pieces of crisply fried rashers of bacon or with roughly chopped onion fried separately in butter till golden.

Apples à la
Normande

*Apples
Butter
Breadcrumbs*

This way of baking apples comes from Normandy. Core some apples, but do not peel them, and fill up their centres with fresh butter. Sprinkle a fireproof dish with brown breadcrumbs (after buttering it, of course), put the apples on this and bake them in the oven, adding more butter from time to time as it is absorbed by the apples. When they are quite done, pour half a teaspoonful of Calvados (if you can get it, for this is the authentic flavouring), or brandy or Maraschino in each centre, powder with sugar and put on top a spoonful of some red jam or jelly, red-currant jelly being the best.

Calvados or Brandy or Maraschino Red-currant jelly

Two ways of baking pears.

One. Wash, but do not peel, some cooking pears, then cook them in the oven in some water with a little sugar and cinnamon. They should cook very slowly indeed. Half-way through their cooking, add a glass of red wine, which should have practically disappeared by the time the pears are ready. Dish them and pour over them what syrup there is left.

Pears
Bonne Femme

Pears Cinnamon Red wine

Two. Peel some pears and cut them into thin slices. Put these into a fireproof dish, adding sugar and little pieces of butter between each layer. Brown in the oven.

Pears
au beurre

Pears Butter Sugar

Apples can be cooked in the same way, they tell me.

We may be lucky and get some early celery at the end of the month. It mixes well with cheese, whether hot or cold. This is the hot one.

Apples
au beurre

Cook some inch-long pieces of celery in slightly salted boiling water. Drain it and stir with a tablespoonful of butter for a minute or so. To this add a cupful of white sauce made with a little milk and some of the water in which the celery was boiled. Season well, add some grated cheese and a teaspoonful of lemon juice. Pour into a dish, sprinkle with more cheese and brown under the grill.

Celery and
Cheese, I

Celery White sauce Cheese Lemon

Celery and Cheese, II

*Celery
Gorgonzola or
Stilton cheese
Butter*

Although we often eat celery with our cheese, this dish may nevertheless surprise our friends. Have some Gorgonzola or Stilton cheese mixed with an equal quantity of butter, and having opened the hearts of two or three good heads of celery, stuff the hollow part of each stick with the mixture. Having done this, press the sticks back so that they will resume their natural shape and serve the heads, in all innocence, on a large flat dish, cutting the pieces across when you want to help them. A few kinds of dry biscuits, and you have a climax to your meal the flavour of which will be appreciated—and your ingenuity commended.

Celery and Cucumber Salad

*Celery
Cucumber
Mayonnaise
Radishes
Hard-boiled egg
Gherkins
Parsley*

Celery makes a good salad with cucumber.

Shred the white part of a head of celery into fine strips, leave it in water for about half an hour, then drain and dry it. Peel the cucumber, cut it into one-and-a-half-inch lengths, and shred it in the same way as the celery. Now mix these together with some salt and pepper and a thinnish mayonnaise sauce, heap the salad in a dish, garnish it with radishes and hard-boiled egg, and sprinkle over it a teaspoonful of finely chopped gherkins and parsley mixed together.

NOVEMBER

THE FOOD OF THE MONTH

Food which is in season all the year round is given in the table on page 19.

Note.—Newcomers are printed in italics.

FISH

Sea Fish

Bloaters	*Cod*
Conger Eel	Dabs
Gurnet	Haddock
Herrings	Ling
Skate	Smelts
	Sprats

River Fish

Eels

Shell Fish

Oysters

MEAT

Pork

POULTRY

Ducks	Geese
	Turkeys

GAME

Blackcock
Capercailzie

Grouse	Hares
Leverets	Partridges
Pheasants	Plovers
Ptarmigan	Quails
Rabbits	Snipe
Teal	Doe Venison
Widgeon	Wild Duck
	Woodcock

VEGETABLES

Jerusalem Artichokes

Aubergines	Broccoli
	Brussels Sprouts
Red Cabbage	Cauliflower
Celeriac	*Celery*
Endive	Horseradish
Parsnips	*Savoys*
	Shallots
	Spanish Onions
Spinach	Watercress

FRUIT

	Apricots
	Cranberries
Medlars	Melons
	Pears

EMPIRE IMPORTED FRESH FRUIT

Apples	Grape Fruit
Oranges	Peaches
Pears	Plums

213

The following recipes are given during this month.

NOVEMBER

We need some consolation for the fogs of November. November food provides it, for it is a kindly month, both to our larders and our appetites. We must pursue our soup studies, for nothing is more welcome on damp and misty evenings than really hot soup. But it must be really hot.

Onion Soup is a great warder-off of colds and chills, and about the easiest in the world to make. Slice half a dozen onions thinly and brown them in butter. Add hot water, salt and plenty of pepper, bring to the boil and continue boiling till the soup is reduced by a quarter. You can eat this either with grated cheese, with small slices of toast on which some cheese has been toasted, or, putting the soup into separate plates add a thin slice or two of

Now the November kitchens fortify us against inclement days

Onion Soup

*Onions
Butter
Water
Grated cheese*

French bread dried in the oven, sprinkle with grated cheese and brown quickly in the oven.

Cabbage Soup

Pickled Pork
Cabbage
Bouquet garni
Carrot
Turnip
Parsley
Garlic

Cabbage makes a good winter soup, which has the merit of providing a second course for breakfast as well, for those who like cold pickled pork. Put a pound of pickled pork in a saucepan of cold water with a *bouquet* of parsley, thyme and bayleaf. Cook this for an hour, and then take out the pork and the *bouquet*. Have ready a carrot and a small turnip cut in small pieces, and a good white cabbage finely shredded. Add these to the liquor from the pork with salt and pepper, and cook for another two hours. About half an hour before the soup is wanted, throw in some chopped parsley, a chopped clove of garlic (if you like it), and a little of the pork also cut up fine. This makes a magnificent soup, especially for a family. And you can have the cold pork for breakfast the next morning.

Cod Crème Gratin

Cod
Duchesse
potatoes
Mornay sauce
Parmesan

We have three new fish this month: carp, cod and sprats. The former is seldom met with in England, though the milt can sometimes be obtained in hotels and restaurants. Cod can very pleasantly be cooked *crème gratin*, for most of us do not share Escoffier's encomiums of this rather uninteresting fish. Boil some cod and divide it into small pieces, skinned and boned, of course. Make a wall of *Duchesse* Potatoes round a dish, and pour a thin layer of Mornay sauce within it. On this lay the pieces of cod and cover them with more sauce, but not up to the edge of the wall or it will bubble over. Sprinkle grated Parmesan cheese over the sauce, and a little butter, and brown quickly in the oven. How much nicer than the usual Fish Pie! Any fish can be treated in this way, and if you want a Dish of Really Superior Appearance, you can make the border of potato with a forcing-bag, and gild the top with yolk of egg.

Sprats require a little care to make them presentable, for we have outgrown the days when we used to fry them on the nursery fire. Here is a recipe which can be applied equally well to sprats or smelts, and to whiting, too, though it will take a little longer to cook. Into a well-buttered fireproof dish put two or three tablespoonfuls of Espagnole sauce to which you have added a mixture of a teaspoonful of fried minced onions, some chopped mushroom parings, salt, pepper, nutmeg and chopped parsley. Lay the fish on this bed, surround them with slices of raw mushrooms, add a tablespoonful or two of white wine and cover with more sauce, on which you sprinkle fine browned breadcrumbs. Cook the whole in the oven till it is *gratinée*, that is, browned, and the fish done, and when serving squeeze over a few drops of lemon juice. A little chopped parsley improves its appearance and flavour.

Whiting
Smelts or
Sprats
au gratin

The Fish
Espagnole
sauce
Onions
Mushrooms
Parsley
Lemon
Nutmeg
White wine
Breadcrumbs

Crabs now go out of season, but lobsters remain all the year round. A grilled one is a change. Get a live one, if you do not object to the business of boiling him, and then three-quarters cook him. Split him, sprinkle him with melted butter and finish cooking under the grill. This should be served with a Devilled Sauce.

Grilled
Lobster

Lobster
Butter

Beef, mutton and pork are all very good now. A goulash of beef, a classic Hungarian dish, is a worthy object of our hungry attention. Cut about three pounds of lean beef into about inch-sized cubes and fry them in a quarter of a pound of lard with half a pound of coarsely chopped onions till the latter are golden. Add a teaspoonful of salt, a

Goulash of
Beef

Beef
Lard
Onions
Tomatoes
Paprika
Potatoes

pound of peeled and quartered tomatoes, a good teaspoonful of paprika and a wineglassful of water. Cover and cook in the oven for an hour and a half. Now add a teacupful of water and a pound of smallish potatoes cut into fours. Cook in the oven again, stirring now and then, for about an hour or until the liquid has disappeared. This is extraordinarily good for a winter's day, for it is hot in two senses of the word.

**Roast Fowl
à l'Allemande**

*Fowl
Chestnuts
Veal stuffing
Sauce with stock
Chipolata
sausages
Lemon*

If the Italian organ-grinder has almost gone the way of the German band, the wayside chestnut-roaster comes out of his lair these days. We will use his wares for roasting a fowl in the German fashion. Cook some chestnuts, about a pound, having parboiled and skinned them. Keep back a dozen or so, and put the remainder into the body of the fowl, which you have stuffed in the ordinary way with veal stuffing. While it is roasting, lightly brown an ounce of flour in an ounce of butter, add a pint of stock, bring to the boil and season. Put in the rest of the chestnuts, simmer for a quarter of an hour, and you have a fine sauce to serve with the fowl, which you will bring to the table garnished with fried chipolata sausages and slices of lemon.

Endives

*Endives
Butter
Lemon*

November increases our list of vegetables by celery and endive, while Jerusalem artichokes take the place of the Globe. Endives, which for some obscure reason are always called chicory in this country, supply a nicely bitter dish when braised. Here is a Belgian way of cooking them. Well butter a flattish saucepan, and lay the endives in it after they have had their outside leaves removed and have been carefully washed. Add a cupful of water, salt and pepper, a few small pieces of butter and a good squeeze of lemon. Cover with a buttered paper and cook them slowly (from half an hour to an hour), turning them once, till they are quite soft but not browned. Thus plain, they can accompany every kind of butcher's meat or, if they are to be served alone, they can be enriched by a Mornay sauce, or served with cream, *hollandaise* or *mousseline* sauces.

This is the month of farewell, indeed, to fruit, but the pretty rosy cranberry will add lustre to our apple pies and puddings. Even the list of Empire fruits is sadly diminished. We must fall back, metaphorically, on puddings made with jam.

Here is a very special one, which used to be the delight of my boyhood. It is called Guards' Pudding, whether from its colour (by which its name would be wrong) or because its deliciousness was only fit for so superior a body of men. Mix well together five ounces of breadcrumbs, three ounces of castor sugar, the same of melted butter, a saltspoonful of carbonate of soda dissolved in a teaspoonful of water, three well-beaten eggs and five tablespoonfuls of raspberry jam. Put it in a buttered mould, and steam for a couple of hours. I believe that strawberry jam may be used, but for me the authentic flavour is of raspberries.

Guards'
Pudding

*Breadcrumbs
Sugar
Butter
Carbonate of
soda
Eggs
Raspberry or
Strawberry
jam*

*   *   *

If we cannot afford the time or the expense of preparing an elaborate Russian *Bortsch*, we can try a more modest Beetroot Soup. Bake three beetroots in water for three hours, then peel them and chop them up with a head of celery. Have a pint of water

Beetroot
Soup

*Beetroots
Celery
Water*

Milk
Cream
Butter

and the same measure of milk in a saucepan, and cook the beetroot and celery in this till they are soft enough to pass through a sieve. Having done this to them, add a spoonful of cream and a little butter, and serve.

Omelettes

Omelettes come to our tables mostly as 'sweet' or 'savoury', and it is hardly realised what an enormous number of different sorts there are. I do not propose to enter into the question of how to cook an omelette, and in this simple operation each must work out his own salvation. Assuming, however, that there is no difficulty about the cooking, let us note a few ways in which omelettes can be presented to us. In some omelettes the flavour is folded in after the omelette is cooked; in others it is incorporated into the mixture before it is put into the pan. Let us take the 'sweet' omelettes first.

Liqueur
Omelettes

Liqueur Omelettes. The omelette should be seasoned with sugar and a little salt, and cooked in the ordinary way. When it is done, dish it, sprinkle with sugar, pour whatever liqueur you fancy over it, and set it alight on coming to the table. Rum is most commonly met with as an adjunct to omelettes, but other liqueurs are very good.

Jam
Omelettes

Jam Omelettes. Season and cook the omelette as above, and when folding put inside it some slightly warm jam. These omelettes can be sprinkled with icing sugar, if liked, and very quickly glazed before serving.

Christmas
Omelette

An amusing variant of this jam omelette, which is suitable for Christmas time, is this: Add to the eggs when beating, two tablespoonfuls of cream, a pinch of orange rind and a tablespoonful of rum, these quantities being for six eggs. Fold into the omelette when it is cooked as much warmed mincemeat as it will safely hold, and sprinkle with heated rum, which you will light as the dish is being served.

Soufflé Omelettes. In this case you beat up the yolks and whites separately. Mix the yolks of three eggs with a quarter of a pound of sugar till smooth, then add by degrees four stiffly-whipped whites. Butter a flat metal or fireproof glass dish and put this mixture on it, giving it the shape of an omelette and seeing that there is some space between it and the edges of the dish to allow for its expansion. Smooth it over and cook in a moderate oven from ten to fifteen minutes, sprinkling it with icing sugar two minutes before you take it out. This omelette can be flavoured with anything you like, the flavouring being added to the yolks before the whites are stirred in.

Soufflé
Omelettes

Now for the 'Savoury' Omelettes, and first those in which the flavouring is folded in as a sort of stuffing. Here are some 'stuffings':

'Savoury'
Omelettes

Asparagus tips tossed in butter.
Artichoke bottoms quartered and tossed in butter.
Chickens' livers tossed in butter.
Soft roes cooked in butter.
Braised endives with cream.
Mushrooms minced and tossed in butter.
Braised lettuce and cream.
Peas *à la française.*
Spinach purée with cream.
Sauté pieces of kidney.
Tomatoes and onions cooked in butter.

A larger number of omelettes are made by mixing the ingredients with the beaten eggs. The omelette is then cooked in the usual way.

Mushrooms minced and tossed in butter.
Very small dice of crust fried in butter.
Very small pieces of lean ham, or tongue.
Fines Herbes, that is, finely chopped parsley, chervil, chives and tarragon.
Half an onion finely minced and cooked in butter, and chopped parsley.
Little *sauté* potato cubes and chopped parsley.
Grated cheese.

Cooked mussels tossed in butter with a little onion and some parsley.

Fried cubes of bacon, spring onions and parsley chopped together, and perhaps a suspicion of garlic.

Pimentoes cut in small pieces and tossed in butter or pork fat. And so on.

Cream Omelette

Eggs
Mushrooms
Cream
Béchamel sauce
Cheese

But here are a couple of omelettes which deserve your special attention.

The first is a Cream Omelette. Cook the omelette as usual, and fold into it a few fresh mushrooms cooked in cream and butter. Then pour over it a thin well-seasoned Béchamel sauce to which you have added some cream and grated cheese, and brown lightly under the grill. The success of this omelette depends on the rapidity with which you can cover it with sauce and brown it. It will help matters considerably if the omelette is not too well done before the last operation is performed.

Smoked Haddock Omelette (Omelette Arnold Bennett)

Eggs
Smoked haddock
Cream
Sauce Mornay
Cheese

The second is an omelette named after Arnold Bennett and to be found in the Savoy Grill:

Add a finely chopped fillet of smoked haddock with a little cream to your eggs, add also some pepper, and cook the omelette, but not too much. Do not fold it, but turn it out flat on a dish, coat it with a little Sauce Mornay, sprinkled with grated cheese, and brown quickly under the grill.

Cod à la Portugaise

Cod
Olive oil
Onion

This is the Portuguese way of cooking Cod:

Lay two steaks of fresh cod, weighing about half a pound each, in a saucepan where you have already put a good piece of butter, a tablespoonful of olive oil, an onion finely chopped and lightly fried, a tiny piece of bruised garlic, a pinch or two of coarsely chopped parsley, four small peeled, 'de-pipped' and chopped tomatoes, and a *bouquet* of parsley, thyme and bayleaf. Add a good glass of white wine and cook with the lid on over the flame for five minutes. Then take off the lid and complete the cooking at the side of the fire, or on a very low gas, for a quarter of an hour. Arrange the slices on a dish, and pour over them the sauce from which you have removed the *bouquet* at the last moment.

Garlic
Parsley
Tomatoes
Thyme
Bayleaf
White wine

A young friend of mine, whose wife was in despair at the sudden arrival of some guests to dinner, told me that she regaled them in the end with the following dish of sole. It was composed quite *impromptu* on her part, and I cannot find a name for it in any of my books of reference, though I have no doubt it has been invented by many others. It had better remain nameless, as far as I am concerned, unless it may be called 'C. M.'

Sole with Cheese and Bananas, 'C. M.'

Fillets of sole
Béchamel sauce
Gruyère
Parmesan
Potato purée
Egg
Bananas

Lay some fillets of sole in a buttered dish. Cover them with stock made from the trimmings, and add two or three very small pieces of butter. Poach it gently in the oven. Meanwhile you have cooked a pint of Béchamel sauce with a quarter of a pint of the fish stock. Having let this reduce by half, you have added to it two ounces of grated Gruyère cheese and the same of Parmesan. Now in the dish in which the fillets are to be served, pour a layer of the sauce. Surround this with a wall of potato purée, which you will brush over with beaten egg yolk. Lay the fillets on the sauce and surmount each with a thin long slice of banana previously cooked in a little fresh butter. Pour over a very little more sauce, sprinkle with cheese, and brown the whole quickly in the oven.

It may be useful here to give a recipe for a really fine Fish Stock or *Fumet*.

Fish Fumet

Onion

Parsley
Fish trimmings
Lemon
White wine
Water

Butter the bottom of a stewpan and put in a blanched onion cut in slices, one or two parsley roots or some parsley stalks, and the trimmings and bones of any fish suitable for the purpose. Add the juice of half a lemon, cover the stewpan, leave it on the fire and shake it occasionally. Now add a quarter of a bottle of Chablis, take the lid off and reduce the liquid by fierce boiling to about half. When this is done, add a pint and a half of cold water, bring to the boil, skim and cook for twenty minutes only on a moderate fire.

The use of a *fumet* of this kind will add distinction to any dish.

Potted Sprats

Sprats
Bayleaves
Mace
Onion
Nutmeg
Vinegar

Soused Herring and Mackerel are quite familiar to us. Potted Sprats sound, and are, a little more elegant.

Take off the heads and tails, dry them and put them in a fireproof dish. Sprinkle with salt and pepper, and add two bayleaves, a blade of mace, a chopped onion and a little grated nutmeg. Pour over the fish enough vinegar to cover them, add one or two small pats of butter and bake in a moderate oven for twenty minutes or half an hour. Quite a nice cold dish for those who do not dislike vinegar.

Lobster à l'américaine

Lobster
Oil
Butter
Carrots
Onions
Brandy
White wine
Curry powder

Many are quite passionately devoted to Lobster *à l'américaine*—and rightly, too, I think. It is not a difficult dish to make.

Cook in a saucepan with a tablespoonful of olive oil and a level tablespoonful of butter, two or three carrots and the same number of onions, chopped of course. Cook for five minutes, when you will add the flesh of two or three small lobsters cut in not-too-small pieces. Cook for another five minutes, then throw in a liqueur-glassful of brandy, which you will light and let burn for a few moments. Now add a glassful of white wine, some curry powder and cayenne pepper at your discretion, salt, chopped parsley and a good spoonful of tomato purée. Cover and cook for an hour on a moderate flame. A few minutes before serving add a little more brandy and white wine. Your remembrance of the last dish you had will help you with the spicy ingredients, which should on no account be stinted.

Cayenne
Parsley
Tomato purée

For a very simple little dish, try this one.
Make a nice white sauce with butter, flour and three-quarters of a pint of milk, and season it with salt, cayenne, a little mace, and a few drops of anchovy essence. Cook a little and add a pint of picked shrimps. Warm well through, and serve.

Shrimps
Czarina

Shrimps
Béchamel sauce
Cayenne
Mace
Anchovy
essence

This is rather an unusual way of frying raw minced beef.
Fry a chopped onion in butter, and add a pound of fresh-minced meat and enough stock to moisten it. Take it off the fire, add a little cream, salt and pepper. Shape into rounds and fry them in butter. They should be served on *croûtons* of fried bread, surmounted by a small spoonful of horseradish sauce.

Fried Minced
Beef

Onion
Raw beef
Stock
Cream
Horseradish
sauce

A Mutton Pudding can be made in the same way as a Beefsteak Pudding. Add a little kidney, which will be found to be a great improvement. I fancy some will like the addition of a little onion, too.

Mutton
Pudding

This is Sausages *en surprise*. Broil some sausages and let them get cold. Make a purée of potato and beat an egg into it. Wrap each sausage, skinned, if you please, in this purée, and egg-and-breadcrumb and fry them. Or you can bake them in the oven,

Sausages
en surprise

Sausages
Potato purée
Egg

Egg and breadcrumbs

gilding the potato. The long, thin sausages are the best for this, or even the diminutive chipolatas.

Escalopes de veau

Veal cutlets (or *escalopes de veau*) make a useful dish for all occasions. With their various garnishes they have an air of distinction about them which it is hard for the hostess, or the guests, to resist. May I suggest a few garnishes?

> Fried in egg and breadcrumbs and garnished with chopped parsley, hard-boiled egg and anchovy fillets.
> With macaroni bound with grated cheese and tomato purée.
> With little heaps of freshly-cooked vegetables.
> With peas *à la française*.
> With a purée of spinach.
> With quartered mushrooms tossed in butter.
> With various sauces, particularly with a paprika sauce (which, by the way, is delicious with sole).

Kromeskis

Cooked meat
Chicken or veal
Ham or Tongue
Onion
Mushrooms
Béchamel sauce
Egg
Bacon
Batter

Kromeskis are another adornment to a meal, and a very useful way of employing cold meat. Cut up the meat, chicken or veal into very small pieces and mix them with some little bits of ham or tongue, a little onion and some chopped mushrooms tossed in butter, with a little thick Béchamel sauce, so that they are nicely bound together. Add the yolk of an egg, and spread out to cool. When this mixture is cold, shape it into small rolls and wrap each in a very thin rasher of streaky bacon. Dip them in fritter batter and fry them golden. Fish may also be used on occasion to form the stuffing, and the flavouring of the sauce can, of course, be varied.

There are a number of ways of cooking pheasant which are not familiar to us in England, but they are, most of them, too complicated for such simple cookery as is advocated here. It might be worth

226

while remembering, however, that pheasant can be very good when boiled and served with an oyster or celery sauce, while braised pheasant comes within measurable distance of the roast.

Put half a clove of garlic, some powdered herbs and salt and pepper inside the pheasant, which you will now place in a *cocotte* with an ounce and a half of butter. Brown the bird in this, add some good stock, cover the *cocotte* and put it in the oven. Take out the garlic after you have finished your frying, cook the pheasant for three-quarters of an hour, and serve with a purée of chestnuts.

*Braised
Pheasant*

*Pheasant
Garlic
Powdered
herbs
Stock
Chestnut purée*

Rabbit is a rather more modest dish than his feathered neighbour, but he makes a very excellent purée.

Bone a young rabbit, pound the flesh and sieve it finely. Season with salt, pepper, a pinch of nutmeg, a little tomato sauce, some good white stock. Put it all in a saucepan and boil it till it is of the same consistency as cream. Eat it with fried *croûtons*. A few small braised onions would do no harm with it.

*Purée of
Rabbit*

*Rabbit
Nutmeg
Tomato sauce
White stock
and possibly
Onions*

Stuffed Cabbage is a meat and vegetable course in one.

Boil a large white cabbage in salt water for a quarter of an hour, then take it out, drain it, and open the leaves without breaking them. Now stuff it just plainly between the leaves with sausagemeat or, if you prefer it, a more elaborate farce of veal, bacon, garlic, parsley, thyme, sage and breadcrumbs all bound together with an egg. Close the cabbage up and tie it with string. Put it into a fireproof dish with a good piece of butter, two or three spoonfuls of stock, salt and pepper, and bake it in a moderate oven, basting it well.

*Stuffed
Cabbage*

*Cabbage
Sausagemeat
or Veal
Bacon
Garlic
Parsley
Thyme
Sage
Breadcrumbs
Egg
Stock*

Potato
Beignets

*Potatoes
Cream
Eggs
Frying fat*

Potato *beignets* can be served either as an accompaniment to a meat dish, or separately as a sweet. Mash some boiled potatoes with an ounce of butter, a pinch of salt (and if they are to be sweet, a little sugar), and a tablespoonful of cream. Mix well till smooth, adding two or more eggs, one by one, till the mixture is stiff enough to be made into little balls, which you can then roll in flour and fry in deep fat, powdering them, if you wish, with a little more sugar. They can be made rather lighter if the yolks are first added and the whites whipped and folded in. In this case no cream should be added.

Duchesse
Potatoes

*Potatoes
Egg
Nutmeg*

Duchesse Potatoes are always exceedingly useful for a garnish.

Mash some potatoes, adding a yolk of egg to every quarter of a pound, and stir to a smooth paste with a little butter. Add salt, pepper and grated nutmeg. Shape the mixture into squares on a floured board, gild them with yolk of egg and bake them in the oven. This mixture is often used for the decoration of dishes by means of a forcing-bag.

Potatoes
Duchesse au
Chester

*Same as above
and Cheese*

Potatoes *Duchesse au Chester* are made by simply adding grated cheese to the mixture above.

Potatoes
Marquise

See Duchesse.
*Tomato
Purée*

Potatoes *Marquise* are also made from the same mixture, with the addition of a little thick tomato purée. Both these latter are baked in the oven in the same way as the *Duchesse* potatoes.

Apples
Flambées

*Apples
Calvados*

Last month I recommended cooking apples and flavouring them with Calvados. If you were able to get any of this liqueur, here is another way of using it.

Peel and quarter some eating apples, and cook them very carefully in fresh butter in a frying-pan till they are soft and brown on each side. Sprinkle them with castor sugar, pour over a glass of Calvados, set it alight, and serve as the flame dies down.

Orange Fritters can be advantageously *flambées*, too.

Orange
Fritters

*Batter
Brandy
Oranges*

Make some pancake batter to which you have added a liqueur-glassful of brandy. Set it aside for two or three hours. Cut the oranges into sections, removing the skin, pips and pith. For each section put two tablespoonfuls of the batter into a cup, put in the section and pour it out with the batter into the frying-pan. Fry for a few minutes and keep it hot.

Now is the exciting moment, which will transform your fritter from the ordinary workaday one. Put all the fritters into a chafing dish (or a pan on the lowest of low flames), pour over a very small glassful of brandy, and set it alight. You may want to add a little sugar, but it is really unnecessary unless you have a very sweet tooth. This is a very delicious dish, and could be used with great effect at a chafing-dish supper, for instance, as the batter would be all the better for keeping.

Peaches can, of course, be *flambées* with various liqueurs, Kirsch perhaps being the most popular. Either warm the peach through in the chafing dish, or poach it till soft in water with sugar and a vanilla pod. When it is ready, dredge it with a little fine sugar, pour over your Kirsch, or whatever liqueur you have chosen, and set it alight. It is just as well to warm the liqueur slightly, as then it catches fire more quickly; and, if you take my advice, you will have your peach poached.

Peaches
Flambées

*Peaches
Vanilla pod
Kirsch or other
liqueur*

**Peaches
with
White Wine**

*Peaches
White wine*

Here is another way of cooking peaches, which
may be served hot or cold. Peel and cut the peaches
in half, remove the stones and marinate the fruit for
about an hour in a claret-glassful of Sauterne. Now
take out the peaches and fry them very lightly in
two ounces of butter in a stewpan. Drain them, and
make a syrup with sugar of the wine in which they
were marinated, adding the kernels to it. When this
is ready, pour it over the fruit.

**Pancakes,
Crêpes
Flambées**

Pancakes are perhaps more suitable for winter
eating than for those spring days in which Shrove
Tuesday falls. I have already described one or two
superfine ones. Let us now turn our attention to the
humbler sort.

It is very seldom that they appear to us in any
other shape than a dull roll of batter with a squeeze
of lemon juice. Even orange juice is a change. But
crêpes flambées are a revelation. When the pancakes
are made, warm them through again in a pan with
a little butter and some crushed sugar rubbed on
lemon or orange skin, fold them in four, pour over
them whatever liqueur your fancy dictates, set it
alight and serve. A little brandy added to the liqueur
you choose (provided it has a brandy base) is an
improvement, if this dish can be improved.

Sweet pancakes can, of course, be stuffed with
jam or with various fruit purées.

**Savoury
Pancakes**

But just as omelettes can be sweet or savoury, so
can pancakes, though this is seldom realised. You
can, indeed, stuff them with almost anything, sweetbreads, asparagus tips, peas, caviare (in the Russian
manner), or various chopped and seasoned meats.
This method of serving them demands, of course, a
batter from which the sugar has been omitted. A

sauce is often an improvement; for example tomato with the sweetbreads, with the asparagus Béchamel, with perhaps a little grated cheese sprinkled over and browned. There are, in fact, so many ways of presenting pancakes that a Swiss Cookery Book sent to me recently contained forty-six recipes for pancakes alone, and it was a little book intended to be by no means comprehensive.

Why is it that while Toasted Cheese is hailed with such delight in city chophouses, we never have it at home? It cannot be because it is difficult to prepare.

There are alternative ways of cooking it, and here they are.

If you have not got a cheese-toaster (and I expect there are very few who have one nowadays), use a chafing-dish or a small metal dish which you can cook over a saucer of water. Cut some cheese into thin slices, put them in the dish, spread on them some mustard, and add a little butter broken into small pieces and some pepper of the kind you prefer. Pour two tablespoonfuls of ale or stout over the cheese (the principles of some may demand milk instead—which may be granted), and put the dish into a fairly hot oven till the cheese is melted. Some melt it under a low grill, for like myself they prefer the top slightly browned. But all serve it with dry toast handed separately.

The other way of cooking it is much simpler. Toast some slices of bread, butter them and spread a little mustard on them. Cover each piece of toast with slices of cheese which have already been toasted on one side, with the toasted side downwards, place the pieces under a grill or in a pretty hot oven, and

Toasted Cheese, I

*Cheese
Mustard
Ale
Stout or Milk*

Toasted Cheese, II

*Cheese
Mustard
Toasted bread*

serve when the cheese is done. I have found that if the grill is used it is better to use grated cheese, or the toast will get too hard. Let the cayenne pepper pot be near at hand.

Good wives, please note.

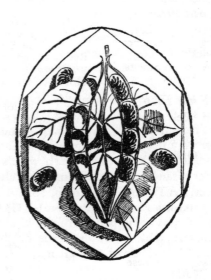

DECEMBER

THE FOOD OF THE MONTH

Food which is in season all the year round is given in the table on page 19.

Note.—Newcomers are printed in italics.

FISH

Sea Fish

Bloaters	Cod
Dabs	Gurnet
Haddock	Ling
Skate	Smelts
Sprats	

River Fish

Eels

Shell Fish

Oysters

MEAT

Pork

POULTRY

Ducks	Geese
Turkeys	

GAME

Capercailzie

Grouse	Hares
Leverets	Partridges
Pheasants	Plovers
Ptarmigan	Quails
Rabbits	Snipe
Teal	Doe Venison
Widgeon	Wild Duck
Woodcock	

VEGETABLES

Jerusalem Artichokes
Broccoli
Brussels Sprouts

Red Cabbage	Celeriac
Celery	Endive
Horseradish	Parsnips
Salsify	Savoys

Shallots
Spanish Onions
Spinach

FRUIT

Apricots
Cranberries

Medlars	Pears

EMPIRE IMPORTED FRESH FRUIT

Apples	Apricots
Grape Fruit	Oranges
Peaches	Pears
Plums	

The following recipes are given during this month:

DECEMBER

We are approaching our farewell to the year, a leave-taking transfigured by the glories and festivities of Christmas. At no other time does the Englishman let himself go so generously, and imbued with a Saturnalian spirit he abandons himself to one short orgy of eating. Never have the tradesmen such unlimited supplies, or such easy credit: never has the larder seemed so infinitesimally small. Even the most careless housewife gives at last some thought to her catering, and does her best to vie with her, and his, relations in providing a really bumper Christmas meal. For her reputation is at stake both for discrimination and hospitality.

Our food supplies remain much the same as in November. Salsify is added to the shopping list,

December, presaging the year's farewell, surpasses the earlier months with Christmas hospitality, and sends us on our way rejoicing

while conger eel, herrings, blackcock and cauliflower are removed from it. We shall have taken the precaution to earmark our turkey in good time, and no one shall dispute with us the cooking of it. He shall be roast, not boiled or braised, though there is a good deal to be said for each of these methods. His stuffing admits, I agree, of variation. Most will demand the sausagemeat hallowed by use; others will vote for chestnuts, some for chestnuts and sausagemeat combined: but on no table of mine shall he appear with his inside crammed with chestnuts and his poor crop bulging hoggishly with pork. Even at this season of gastronomic licence we can be too lavish, and monstrosities are worse at the table than anywhere. The adventurous, however, may like to try something new, so here is a stuffing for roast turkey which is eaten in some parts of Italy.

Italian Turkey Stuffing

Sausages
Chestnuts
Prunes
Pears
Turkey's liver
White wine
Butter

Half cook half a pound of chipolata sausages, let them get cold, skin them and cut them into round slices. Also boil and peel half a pound of chestnuts, and scald half a dozen French prunes which you will then stone and halve. Melt two ounces of butter in a saucepan, and in this cook for a few minutes the pieces of sausage, the chestnuts, the prunes, the skinned and cored quarters of four pears and the turkey's liver blanched and coarsely chopped. Strain off the butter and pour in a glass of white wine, and stuff your turkey with this intriguing mixture.

But if our turkey should not be overwhelmed with stuffing, we can add to the delights of his consumption by handing separately all kinds of cunning extras, chestnuts braised in a rich gravy or in a purée with cream, some curly bacon grilled or fried, a scattering of mushrooms, little sausages, tiny balls of forcemeat, and even truffles. And as an alternative to our Christmas pudding accompanied by whipped cream into which a little old brandy has been beaten, let us have a large flat covered mince pie, so much more luscious than those usual pielets whose flaky pastry always harbours too little of the juicy home-made mincemeat.

Goose we should have some time at Christmastide, if only to eat up his remains in a masterly stew which hails from that part of France where goose is understood! Brown the pieces in goose fat and, having taken them out, cook in the same fat a couple of thinly sliced onions and a slice of raw ham or bacon cut in small dice. Skin four tomatoes and remove the pips, cut them up and add them, with a *bouquet* of parsley, thyme and bayleaf, to the onion and ham. Pour in three cupfuls of beef stock, or water, liberally seasoned with pepper and some salt, bring to the boil and cook for a quarter of an hour. Now remove the *bouquet*, and simmer for two hours. The remains of turkey, chicken or duck can be disposed of in the same way, and if you have no goose fat, then bacon fat is permissible, though not quite so good.

Ragout of Turkey, Goose, Chicken or Duck

The remains of the bird
Onions
Ham or bacon
Tomatoes
Bouquet garni
Beef stock
Goose or bacon fat

Cold Turkey demands a Cranberry Sauce. Dissolve enough sugar in water to make a thickish syrup, boil it for ten minutes and then add half a pint of cranberries. Put on the lid and cook very gently (so that the berries do not burst) till they are tender and transparent, skimming now and then. This sauce is better if you make it the day before you want to use it.

Cranberry Sauce (Cold)

Cranberries
Sugar

The main Christmas dishes are at our fingers' ends: it is often the adjuncts to the many meals that perplex us. Potted shrimps always provide a very

Potted Shrimps

Shrimps

Butter
Mace
Cayenne
Nutmeg

delicious stand-by, and they will keep quite well. Into a saucepan in which you have melted three or four ounces of butter put a pint of large shelled shrimps, a blade of mace pounded up, as much cayenne as your palate will bear and, if you care for it, some grated nutmeg. Heat them up slowly and do not let them boil. Pour them into little pots, glasses or *cocottes* (you will serve one to each guest), and cover with melted butter.

Petits pots
de crème

Milk
Eggs
Sugar
Flavouring

Another stand-by, this time a sweet, are *petits pots de crème*, an invention, I believe, of the eighteenth century. Fill eight little pots with milk, and put it all into a saucepan with three ounces of sugar and the flavouring you have chosen. Boil it up and let it get cold. Now beat up the yolks of six eggs (your potted ones will do at a pinch), add them to the milk and pass through a hair sieve. With this fill the pots and cook them in the oven in a baking-dish of water till they are set, which will take about twenty minutes. They are, of course, served cold, and it is difficult to persuade your guests that they are not made with cream. Almost any flavour can be used, vanilla, coffee, chocolate, lemon, orange, even tea. They can also be made with plain black coffee instead of milk, but they may be a little watery this way.

Marrons
Glacés

Chestnuts
Sugar
Lemon

Marrons glacés give a touch of distinction to any dessert, and, though they are expensive to buy, they can be made quite simply as follows. Peel and boil as many chestnuts as you will want. Clarify some sugar and boil the chestnuts in it for a few minutes. Then coat them thickly with sugar, brown them in the oven and at the last minute squeeze a few drops of lemon juice over them.

If you have made the *pots de crème*, your egg

DECEMBER

whites will come in useful for making méringues, the easiest thing in the world. Do not forget that their cream filling can be improved by the addition of a flavouring. Cherry jam makes a particularly delicious one.

A Swiss manner of serving them is good and picturesque. Make the méringues of different sizes and put a layer at the bottom of a dish. Pour over a mixture of melted chocolate and whipped cream, then another layer of méringues, and so on till the dish is full. On the last layer of cream and chocolate sprinkle a good dusting of chopped roasted almonds.

Méringues à la suisse

Méringues
Chocolate
Cream
Almonds

And so Christmas is over, the company broken up, and with the last day of December comes to an end our journey together through the year's monthly food, and another cycle begins. If only a tithe of the suggestions I have made are useful, I shall be well rewarded. Resting on the laurels which our kitchens have gained during the twelvemonth and ourselves crowned not with bays, but with a fragrant wreath of parsley, thyme and bayleaf, let us look with confidence towards greater culinary triumphs in the year to come. It remains for me to wish my readers a happy gastronomic New Year. May their appetites be sharpened, their zest for the pleasures of the table increase, and their digestions remain unimpaired!

*   *   *

Mushroom Soup will be a pleasant luxury in a month when luxuries may occasionally be permitted. Chop up half a pound of fresh mushrooms with a slice of onion. Simmer this in two pints of

Mushroom
Soup

Mushrooms
Onion

White stock
Flour
Butter
Milk
Cream
and possibly
White wine

white stock for twenty minutes, and pass it through a sieve. Thicken this purée with flour and butter, season it well and add a cupful of half milk, half cream. If you like you can add half a wineglassful of Sauterne at the last minute.

Fried Eggs

It is a shock to some to be told that they do not know what a fried egg is; but it is probably true. The real fried egg is fried in oil, and it looks nothing like the fried egg as we know it so well with our bacon. Try frying one—properly—and see. Heat some oil in a frying-pan till it begins to smoke, then slide the egg, which you have already broken on to a plate and seasoned, into the pan. With a wooden spoon quickly draw the uncooked white over the yolk. The whole thing only takes about half a minute. It looks more like a fritter than anything else.

Eggs fried in this way can be served with rashers of bacon, peas and potatoes; with tomatoes stuffed with rice; with fried slices of aubergine and fried parsley; with a purée of spinach to which have been added a few dice of anchovy fillets.

Poached eggs can also be egg-and-bread-crumbed or dipped in batter and fried, but this is rather a *tour de force* for the amateur.

Scrambled
Eggs

Scrambled or buttered eggs can be treated, so far as garnishes are concerned, in the same way as eggs *en cocotte* or *sur le plat*.

Scotch
Woodcock

Eggs
Buttered toast
Anchovy paste

One special mixture must not be forgotten, the admirable one which constitutes Scotch Woodcock. Butter the eggs and place them on hot buttered toast spread with anchovy paste. Sprinkle a few chopped capers and a little parsley on each. This makes a lovely savoury, and is often acceptable for breakfast—by the most reluctant.

Scrambled eggs with cheese, with tomatoes, with mushrooms, shrimps, chickens' livers, asparagus tips, flaked smoked fish, little fried crusts . . . all are excellent. And to amuse the children eggs can be emptied out without breaking the shells too much, and the shell filled again with scrambled egg.

Capers
Parsley

This is a Creole fashion of cooking fresh cod.

Bone the fish and soak it for half an hour, turning it twice or thrice, in a tablespoonful of olive oil, the same of vinegar, a good squeeze of lemon juice and a tablespoonful of chopped shallot or onion. Butter a fireproof dish, put in the fish and pour over it the mixture in which it has been soaked, adding half a pint of tomato purée, a tablespoonful of chopped green pimento (if you have it) and a seasoning of pepper and salt. Cover the dish and bake in a moderate oven for about three-quarters of an hour. When it is done, sprinkle with a little grated cheese and brown under the grill.

Cod à la
créole

Cod
Olive oil
Vinegar
Lemon
Shallot or
Onion
Tomato purée
Pimento
Cheese

An American fashion of serving grilled sole will be attractive at a little luncheon.

Grill the sole in the usual way, and serve it on a very hot dish and surround it at the last moment with half a dozen oysters poached in a little Worcester sauce. Sprinkle some very hot fried breadcrumbs over the fish, and add a pinch of chopped parsley.

Grilled Sole à
l'américaine

Sole
Oysters
Worcester
sauce
Breadcrumbs
Parsley

This is a charming manner of cooking a small turbot. Place it in a fireproof dish and pour over it some melted butter. Sprinkle with parsley, thyme and chives finely chopped together, and season with

Turbot à la
tartare

Turbot
Butter

243

Parsley
Thyme
Chives
Egg and
breadcrumbs
Tartare sauce

salt and freshly ground black pepper. After it has been left for an hour, brush a beaten egg over it, add some breadcrumbs, and bake in the oven till it is done. Serve with Tartare sauce, from which this method derives its name of Turbot *à la tartare*.

Lobster
à la russe

Lobster
Mayonnaise
Aspic jelly
Salade russe
Hard-boiled eggs
Caviare
Fish jelly
Truffle

Lobster *à la russe* may be very welcome at one of the many meals at Christmas time when cold dishes are in demand. We shall not attempt to aspire to the many operations by which this famous dish is arrived at, but we will cut our cold lobster into slices and coat each with a mixture of mayonnaise sauce and aspic jelly. Having dotted each of these with a little lobster coral, we shall arrange them according to the fancy (or means) of the moment with some *salade russe*, halves of hard-boiled eggs stuffed with caviare, and little rounds of fish jelly surmounted by a piece of truffle.

Salade russe

Salade russe is very simply made by cutting equal quantities of carrots, potatoes, French beans, peas, capers, gherkins, sliced cooked mushrooms, lobster and lean ham into thin *julienne* strips, adding a few anchovy fillets cut in pieces and binding with a mayonnaise sauce. A garnish of beetroot and caviare may be added.

Tournedos

Tournedos, which are really the 'kernel' of a fillet of steak, are one of the most popular dishes there are, in witness whereof Escoffier gives nearly seventy ways of presenting them. They are usually grilled, and then served according to the various designations.

Tournedos
Béarnaise

Tournedos *Béarnaise* are one of the most delicious. The tournedos are grilled and served with potatoes cooked in butter and a Béarnaise sauce.

DECEMBER

Tournedos *à la niçoise* are fried tournedos surmounted by half a tablespoonful of chopped tomato, tarragon and a very little garlic tossed in butter, and served surrounded by small separate heaps of French beans and small potatoes.

Tournedos à la niçoise

Tournedo *Rossini* are probably not so well known to the palate as the music of their creator to the ear. They are fried in butter and dished upon fried bread. On each is placed a slice of *foie gras* which has been floured and fried in butter: and on each slice of *foie gras* is placed a slice of truffle. They are very rich, but very good indeed.

Tournedos Rossini

Here is another method of using up cold roast mutton. Toss the pieces of cold mutton in a little butter. In a separate pan cook also in butter two or three shallots (or onions) finely chopped. When these are browning add them to the mutton, as well as a rasher of bacon cut into little pieces, some chopped parsley, salt and pepper. Then pour in a glassful of dry white wine, and simmer for about half an hour.

Mutton à la bordelaise

Cooked mutton
Shallots
or Onions
Bacon
Parsley
White wine

This is something quite different. The contrast rather aptly illustrates the difference between the *bourgeois* cookery of France and England.

Skin some sausages, cut them in half lengthwise and lay half of them in a buttered pie-dish. Sprinkle them with fried sliced onion and slices of raw peeled tomatoes. Season, add the remainder of the sausages, cover with stock and with a thick layer of mashed potatoes. Dot with butter and brown in the oven.

Sausage and Tomato Pie

Sausages
Onions
Tomatoes
Stock
Potatoes

Another simple dish, a *fricassée* of veal (or chicken, of course).

Make a sauce of butter, flour and veal stock, flavoured with pepper, salt and a pinch of nutmeg.

Fricassée of Veal

Butter
Flour

Veal stock
Nutmeg
Cooked veal
Cream
Parsley
Egg
Lemon

Put in some small pieces of cold cooked veal and let it warm through, but do not boil. Add a little cream, stir well again, and just before serving stir in some finely chopped parsley and an egg-yolk beaten with a good squeeze of lemon juice.

Some cooked green peas or mushrooms cut in pieces and tossed in butter may be added, and the *fricassée* may be garnished with small baked tomatoes, rolls of fried bacon or *croûtons* of fried bread.

Stuffed
Chicken's
Legs

*Cooked chicken's
Legs
Oil
Bacon
Farce as below*

Cold Chicken Legs are usually devilled as a convenient method of disposal. Stuffed and baked legs are more uncommon.

Joint the legs and separate the drumsticks. Marinate them in oil, salt and pepper. Drain them and cover them with the farce described below, wrap each in a slice of bacon, tie them up or skewer them and bake them in the oven for about twenty minutes. Dish up on slices of toast.

Farce for
Stuffed
Chicken's
Legs

*Breadcrumbs
Lemon
Onion
Sweet herbs
Parsley
Cayenne
Egg*

The Farce is composed as follows: two tablespoonfuls of breadcrumbs, half a teaspoonful of finely chopped lemon rind, two slices of onion blanched and finely chopped, half a teaspoonful of chopped sweet herbs, a teaspoonful of chopped parsley seasoned with salt and cayenne pepper and bound with an egg-yolk.

Rabbit
Pudding

*Rabbit
Pickled pork
Suet paste*

One last Pudding, this time of Rabbit. Keep back the head, neck, liver and kidneys; cut the rest of the rabbit into neat pieces. Rub the pieces with a mixture of flour, salt and pepper, and put them in the paste-lined pudding-basin interspersed with cubes of pickled pork, and proceed as usual. Send to the table with gravy made from the head and other parts.

DECEMBER

Potato *croquettes* are made from the same kind of purée as is required for *Duchesse* potatoes. Make little balls of the mixture, roll them in flour, egg-and-breadcrumb them and fry them in deep fat. They can also be varied by the addition of cheese or tomato purée to the purée, and make an admirable accompaniment to numerous entrées.

Potato Croquettes

*Potato purée
Egg and
breadcrumbs
Frying fat
and possibly
Cheese*

Potatoes are always a little difficulty at a time when the menu requires careful supervision, as at Christmas time. It is perfectly easy to vary them without undue trouble, and often almost the same dish varied a little in its manner of presentation will give an impression of something entirely different.

For instance, the ordinary method of frying raw potatoes in this country comprises only the two varieties known as 'fried' and 'chips'. Straw potatoes —that is, cut into the thinnest of thin strips and fried —are a pleasing change, especially with game. *Soufflées* potatoes we have already noted. Potatoes cut into long ribbons of the same thickness can also be treated in the same way, and are called *Pommes de Terre Chatouillard*.

Potatoes
Chatouillard

Quite a different way of frying potatoes is to shape them into pieces the size of hazel-nuts (*Noisettes*), of a large olive (*Château*), or into half-inch cubes (*Pont-Neuf*). Sprinkle them with salt and pepper, and cook them gently in butter till they are soft and golden. Serve with chopped parsley scattered over them.

And there are many other ways, which are yours for the seeking.

Potatoes
Noisettes

Potatoes
Château

Potatoes
Pont-Neuf

While we are on the subject of frying, do not let us forget our friend Celery. Cut it into pieces, cross-wise, about three inches in length. Cook them till

Fried Celery

*Celery
Lemon*

Egg and breadcrumbs or Batter

tender in boiling water with a little lemon juice. Drain and dry well. Egg-and-breadcrumb them or dip them in batter, and then fry them. Mostly this is to be used as a garnish to grills, but fried or grilled bacon and fried celery makes a good luncheon or impromptu supper dish.

Stuffed Tomatoes

Tomatoes Peas or Egg Cheese Breadcrumbs

Four months ago we discussed the question of stuffed tomatoes. The weather then demanded that they should be cold. We might very well consider what we can do with them when hot.

The simplest way is to scoop them out and fill them with new peas (tinned) plainly boiled or cooked à la française. Or fill them with beaten egg, grated cheese and just enough breadcrumbs to stop the mixture from getting wet, and bake in the oven.

Tomatoes stuffed à la napolitaine

Tomatoes Butter Flour Cheese Milk

Here is the Neapolitan way. Cut the tomatoes in half, remove the cores and pips, salt and pepper them. Now make a thick sauce with butter, flour, grated cheese and a little milk. Fill the tomatoes with this and bake for half an hour.

Tomatoes stuffed with Eggs

Tomatoes Eggs Cheese Breadcrumbs

Tomatoes can be stuffed with eggs, by cutting off a piece of the top of the tomatoes, scooping out the core and pulp and breaking into each a whole egg. Sprinkle with grated cheese, browned breadcrumbs and a little melted butter, and cook in the oven till the egg is set.

Tomatoes stuffed with Meat

Tomatoes Oil or Butter Breadcrumbs

For a change stuff them with any meat you have over. Cut some large ripe tomatoes in half and scoop out the cores and juice. Put them aside and make a stuffing by cooking gently with a little oil or butter the insides of the tomatoes, salted and peppered, a few fine breadcrumbs soaked in milk, a small onion finely chopped and some cold meat also chopped small. When this is nearly done, put the tomatoes in the oven for a quarter of an hour, then take them out and stuff them with the mixture. Pile it well up in them, sprinkle with browned breadcrumbs and melted butter, and brown in the oven.

Milk
Onion
Cold meat

The Portuguese stuff them with some pilaff rice mixed with chopped tomato, and serve them sprinkled with parsley.

Tomatoes stuffed à la portugaise

Tomatoes
Rice
Parsley

The Provençal fashion is a trifle more complicated, but very savoury. Cut half a dozen tomatoes in half, scoop out their insides and cook the cases in oil, cut side down, till half cooked, then turn them over and cook a little longer. Meanwhile fry two tablespoonfuls of chopped onion in oil, then add four peeled and roughly chopped tomatoes, a pinch of chopped parsley and a crushed clove or garlic, cover and cook for ten minutes. Now add four tablespoonfuls of breadcrumbs soaked in stock, and two pounded anchovies. Stuff the tomatoes, which you have removed to the serving dish, with this mixture, sprinkle them with grated cheese, breadcrumbs and a little oil, and finish in the oven. These tomatoes may be served hot or cold.

Tomatoes à la provençale

Tomatoes
Oil
Onion
Parsley
Garlic
Breadcrumbs
Stock
Anchovies
Cheese

A cold Chocolate *Soufflé* can be made in the same way as the Orange *Soufflé* mentioned in June, but just now many will prefer a hot one.

Chocolate Soufflé

Chocolate
Milk
Butter
Flour
Vanilla essence
Sugar
Eggs

Simmer two ounces of finely grated chocolate with half a pint of milk till the former is dissolved, then add it to an ounce of melted butter with which has been mixed three ounces of flour. Boil this well, let it cool a little and add half a teaspoonful of vanilla essence, two ounces of sugar and the yolks of three eggs one by one. Stir and beat up well, then add lightly the whipped-up whites of three eggs.

Turn into a *soufflé* dish and cook for about three-quarters of an hour.

Chestnut Cake

Chestnuts
Sugar
Vanilla
Almonds
Preserved
fruit

A jolly Chestnut Cake, which is strongly reminiscent of *marrons glacés*, can be made by first boiling two pounds of chestnuts till they are soft, then skinning them and passing them through a sieve. Add to the ensuing purée a thick syrup made with a pound of sugar flavoured with vanilla, and stir it all together till it is a thick paste. By the way, you should put a little of the syrup aside. Now shape the paste on the dish on which it is to be served, decorate it with almonds and preserved fruit, and glacé it with the rest of the syrup about two hours before you want to eat it.

Cheese Tart

Pastry
Gruyère cheese
Egg
Cream

This is a real Cheese Tart, not a Lemon Cheese one.

Make some pastry and put it in a *flan* mould. Cook it for about twenty minutes. Then fill it with a well-beaten mixture of a quarter of a pound of grated Gruyère cheese, an egg and a good cupful of cream. Cook for a quarter of an hour longer, when the contents of the tart should be an exquisite gold colour.

Risotto à la piedmontaise

Onion
Rice
Saffron
Consommé or
Stock
Butter
Parmesan
Cooked ham

There are various ways of making a Risotto, and many have become quite lyrical about this dish. We will satisfy ourselves with a recipe from Piedmont. Fry a medium-sized onion, finely chopped, in butter, and add to it half a pound of uncooked Carolina rice. In my opinion, this should not be washed first, but simply shaken to remove any dust. If your scruples allow you to follow my example, I advise you to do so. Now put the pan on the side of the stove, or on a very low heat, add a pinch or two of saffron, and

let the rice get thoroughly saturated with the butter.
Now add a cupful of *consommé*, or good stock,
cover the rice and let it cook very slowly till the
stock is absorbed. Then add a little more stock, letting that be absorbed in its turn, until you have
added in all about a pint of stock for this quantity
of rice. Stir with a wooden spoon when the stock is
being added, and as a result of your loving care
you should have in the end a compact creamy mass
of rice, in which, however, each grain of rice pre-
serves its 'identity' and does not help to compose
the sloppy agglomeration which usually passes
muster for this Italian dish. Add at the last a few
pieces of fresh butter and some grated Parmesan,
which you stir in, as well as a few small dice of lean
cooked ham.

According to another writer, a Milanese Risotto
is made in the same manner, save that a little wine
and tomato purée should be added before the stock
is put in, and that the risotto can be made 'more
opulent' (a good touch, that!) with mushrooms and
truffles.

We have ended on rather a heavy note, but it is a
famous dish which should become more famous
still, with your help. It is also a dish which is suitable for all times of the year, so perhaps we may
aptly close with it.

A Happy New Year!

Risotto à la milanaise

Onion
Rice
Saffron
Tomato purée
Consommé or Stock
Butter
Parmesan
White wine
Mushrooms and Truffles

*   *   *

A NOTE ON
SAUCES

★

In this chapter I have written down a few sauces of the kind that those who like good food will appreciate and may wish to have by them, for easy reference. Some are mentioned in the body of the book; others are not, but they will all be found good and useful. In the following recipes I have not been guided by simplicity or economy, because a really good sauce is always worth making properly (though the ingenious may be able to find a few short cuts which will still allow the sauce to retain something of its authentic flavour), and if the time and ingredients for its preparation cannot be spared, it is often better to leave it out or to employ a simpler one more suited to the occasion. Neither have I given any sauces for sweets, for these can easily be found in any good cookery book, and, strictly speaking, I suppose they are hardly sauces in the true sense of the word, but more usually syrups or purées.

Sabayon occurs to my mind, however, as a more important sauce for sweets, so perhaps I should give it here.

Sabayon

For a small sauce mix a quarter of a pound of powdered sugar with three egg yolks in a basin. Add half a pint of dry white wine, and whisk it in a pan set in boiling water till it is firm and frothy and about four times its original size. It can be made with milk instead of wine, if desired, and can then be flavoured according to your liking.

SAUCES

It should always be remembered that sauces need careful cooking. They must be smooth and light, and their correct seasoning ascertained by frequent tasting. They cannot be thrown together in a moment, and, needless to say, they should never be lumpy. If they are stirred as they should be, and not cooked too fast, they should be quite free from this intolerable blemish (which, by the way, is equally a crime in potato purée), but straining will always make certain that lumps are absent.

Experience only can tell how the best results can be obtained with the commodities at one's command, and a little adventuring will do no harm. Above all, a sauce should never be so strongly flavoured as to kill the taste of the dish it accompanies, and a proper manipulation of the dish's various ingredients will ensure that the sauce not only sets off the food to its best advantage, but will itself be given its proper value in the meal.

★   ★   ★

Directions for making the following Sauces are given in this book.

SAUCES

★　　　★　　　★

There are a few sauces which may be called 'basic' sauces and will be mentioned in this chapter as ingredients in others. I will give these first. The others will follow in alphabetical order. I assume that my readers are familiar with the word ' *roux*', which denotes the mixture of flour and butter that constitutes the thickening agent. White *roux* is the flour mixed with the butter and not cooked at all before the liquid is introduced, or only for a long enough time to dissipate the disagreeable taste of raw flour. Pale *roux* is cooked until just before the colour begins to change. Brown *roux* until the flour has acquired a light brown colour and smells

Roux

255

SAUCES

slightly nutty. (Slow cooking is of the utmost importance here.)

I also assume that the method of preparing Stock is understood, as the ultimate flavour of the sauce depends so much upon the flavour which the stock adds to it.

Espagnole or Brown Sauce Espagnole or Brown Sauce is much used in the preparation of others. This is a simple way of making it.

Put three carrots and one onion, all cut up, into a pan with some butter and some scraps of meat, game or veal. Cover and cook slowly till the onions are a pale brown, then add a tablespoonful of flour, brown that slightly, too, and then add enough stock to get the required moisture. Stir till it thickens, add a *bouquet* of parsley, thyme and bay, and simmer gently for about an hour. Season and strain. This sauce will keep in ordinary weather for several days, if it is stored in a covered jar.

Half-Glaze Take a quart, or a lesser quantity, of Espagnole Sauce and cook it with an equal quantity of brown stock till it is reduced—in the case of two quarts—to nine-tenths of a quart. Strain and finish off the fire with a tenth of a quart of sherry.

Velouté This sauce is made by adding White Stock to a pale *roux*. A few mushroom parings may be added, if liked, but the flavour of the stock should really be sufficient. Fish *Velouté* is, of course, made with fish stock.

Allemande Sauce This is really a thickened *velouté*, and is made by mixing a pint of *velouté* with half a pint of cold white stock, the yolks of two eggs, a good squeeze of lemon juice and a little mushroom liquor. Stir this till it is reduced by about a third and add a little cream.

This is the familiar White Sauce made with a white *roux* and boiling milk. The perfect Béchamel is achieved by boiling the milk with an onion stuck with cloves, a little grated nutmeg, salt, pepper and thyme. It should cook slowly for about an hour, but many of us will hardly find the time for this perfection, and a perfectly good one can be made in half the time. — **Béchamel Sauce**

One. Quarter four tomatoes and put them in a saucepan with a carrot and an onion finely chopped, salt and pepper, and, if you like, a pinch of basil. Cover with water, bring to the boil and cook well. Sieve it, add brown *roux*, a little good stock, and reduce till fairly thick. — **Tomato Sauce, I**

Two. Make a brown *roux* and add to it some tinned tomato purée, a very little stock, a small piece of butter, salt, pepper and a grating of nutmeg. Simmer for ten minutes or so. (This is if you want to make the sauce in a hurry.) — **Tomato Sauce, II**

Reduce a couple of tablespoonfuls of vinegar, to which you have added a little pepper, till there is half the quantity, and pour into this the yolks of three eggs, salt, and a nice piece of butter which you have previously mixed in a basin. Stir all together over the fire in a pan of boiling water, adding small pieces of butter till it is smooth. It must be served at once. — **Hollandaise Sauce**

Here are a few other sauces of a kind which may be found useful with the various dishes I have mentioned.

SAUCES

Béarnaise Sauce

Cook in a saucepan two shallots (or onions) finely chopped, a little chopped tarragon (or a dash of tarragon vinegar) and a glass of white wine, till it is reduced by a third. Mix the yolks of three eggs with a small piece of butter and a little cayenne pepper, and pour the liquid over them. Sieve, and cook gently in another saucepan till it thickens, taking care not to boil it. Before serving, sprinkle in a very little lemon juice and some chopped parsley. It should be fairly stiff, and is excellent with *tournedos*, for example.

Bercy Sauce

Cook some chopped shallots (or onions) in butter without browning them and moisten them with half white wine and half *velouté* made with fish stock. Reduce and add chopped parsley before serving.

Bordelaise Sauce

This is a simple method. Cook quickly in oil for five minutes two shallots, a small onion and three or four mushrooms all chopped up. Then add a little flour, a tablespoonful of stock, the same of tomato purée, salt, pepper and chopped parsley. This should then be reduced by a quarter and served at once.

Chasseur Sauce

This sauce is rather complicated and expensive, but as we have often enjoyed it, we might as well know how to make it.

Fry half a dozen minced mushrooms in a level dessertspoonful of butter and the same of oil. When they are slightly browned add a small teaspoonful of minced shallots (or onions). Drain off half the fat and add half a pint of white wine and a liqueur-glassful of brandy. Reduce by half, and finish with half a pint of half-glaze, half that quantity of tomato sauce and a tablespoonful of melted meat glaze. Boil for five minutes longer, and just before serving sprinkle in some chopped parsley.

SAUCES

Reduce a pint of half-glaze by about a third, adding while it is reducing about three-quarters of a pint of meat jelly by degrees. Season and add, off the fire, a little Madeira or Port. Stir while it cools, until it is of the right consistency to coat whatever you are preparing.

Chaud-Froid Sauce (Brown)

A White Chaud-Froid Sauce is made by reducing in the same way a pint of *velouté* to which you have added three-quarters of a pint of chicken or veal jelly, and gradually adding half a pint of cream. You can colour this sauce with tomato purée, or if you want a more delicate shade and flavour, with paprika, this variant being known as *Chaud-Froid à l'Aurore*.

Chaud-Froid Sauce (White)

Chaud-Froid Sauce à l'Aurore

This is a Béarnaise Sauce tinted and flavoured with a purée of tomatoes.

Choron Sauce

This sauce has already been described on page 239.

Cranberry Sauce

An admirable cold sauce can be made as follows. Dissolve four tablespoonfuls of red-currant jelly, and add a good glass of port, a teaspoonful of finely chopped and blanched shallots, the same of orange rind cut in *julienne* strips and blanched, the same of lemon rind similarly treated, a teaspoonful of mustard, a little cayenne pepper and powdered ginger, the juice of an orange and the juice of half a lemon. Mix all well together. It is particularly good with cold venison, and with cold mutton, too.

Cumberland Sauce

Fry in a little butter a small onion, two shallots and a little bacon chopped together. Pour in a glass of white wine, a little vinegar, and add a *bouquet* of thyme, parsley and bay. Reduce by a quarter and

Devil Sauce

enrich by the addition of a little white stock and a little tomato purée, and season with salt, pepper and cayenne. Boil for about five minutes and strain. Piquancy can be given by the addition of Harvey Sauce or Escoffier Sauce at the end.

Hungarian Sauce

Fry in butter, without browning them, two table-spoonfuls of chopped onion, seasoned with salt and plenty of paprika. Add a quarter of a pint of white wine and a *bouquet*, reduce by two-thirds and remove the *bouquet*, add a pint of *velouté*, and boil for five minutes. Strain carefully, and before serving add a good piece of butter. This sauce, especially with veal cutlets, will taste even nicer than it looks.

Indienne Sauce

Though Béchamel Sauce flavoured with curry powder often does service for this sauce, the following gives the more authentic flavour, in which the curry should not be too pronounced. Cook a piece of butter the size of a small egg with a tablespoonful of flour till it is well cooked but not brown. Add a good pinch of saffron and of curry powder, and stir and cook a little more. Then add by degrees a large cupful of milk, and season with salt, pepper and grated nutmeg. More milk can be added if it is too thick, or more seasoning if necessary. Make it creamy at the last moment with a little more butter.

Lyonnaise Sauce

Mince enough onion to make two or three table-spoonfuls, and brown them lightly in two ounces of butter. Add a quarter of a pint of white wine, and the same of vinegar, and reduce till the liquid has almost disappeared. Now add a pint and a half of half-glaze and cook for half an hour. The little pieces of onion may be left in, or the sauce may be strained, as you like.

SAUCES

Melt a largeish piece of butter with a coffeespoonful of water and the juice of a lemon. Warm well, add salt and at the last minute some chopped parsley.

Maître d'hôtel Sauce

This has been described on page 26.

Maltese Sauce

Add to a Béchamel Sauce as much grated Gruyère and Parmesan cheese as your palate demands (or Cheddar cheese will do at a pinch). Some add the beaten yolk of an egg, but this is really unnecessary. A touch of cayenne pepper, or paprika, often improves it.

Mornay Sauce

Put into a saucepan the yolks of two eggs, a drop of cold water, salt, pepper and the juice of a quarter of a lemon. Stand the saucepan in a pan of boiling water, and add one by one small pieces of butter, stirring all the time as you would in making a Mayonnaise Sauce. Do not let it get too hot, and go on adding the butter till the sauce is soft and creamy. Do not be upset if the first attempt is a failure, but try again. It is as temperamental as mayonnaise—and as easy to make when once you have the knack.

Mousseline Sauce

Mustard Sauce can be made either by adding mustard to a Hollandaise Sauce, or as follows. Make a butter sauce with half an ounce of butter, the same of flour and half a pint of boiling water. When this is mixed, but not boiling, add the yolks of two eggs, a little cream and the juice of half a lemon. Finish with more butter and about a dessertspoonful of mustard.

Mustard Sauce

A third way is to stir a dessertspoonful of flour into an ounce of melted butter, adding salt, pepper, a tablespoonful of dry mustard, a teaspoonful of vinegar and a little water. Stir on a slow heat till it thickens, and thank God for it and fine fresh herrings!

Orange Sauce

Cut the rind of an orange into thin *julienne* strips and cook them for five minutes in boiling water. Drain them and add to them a cupful of Espagnole Sauce, pepper, salt and the juice of two oranges and one lemon. Stir till very hot.

Paprika Sauce

This is the same as the Hungarian Sauce already described.

Piquante Sauce

Put two chopped shallots into a saucepan with a *bouquet* and three tablespoonfuls of vinegar (or fifty fifty white wine and vinegar). Reduce it to a third and add some stock or gravy. Mix in a brown *roux*, cook a little longer and, when you have seasoned it to your liking, add some chopped gherkins, capers and parsley and freshly ground black pepper.

Portuguese Sauce

Fry some chopped onion lightly in oil. Add some coarsely chopped peeled tomatoes, salt, freshly ground pepper, tomato sauce, a little garlic, chopped parsley and a little meat glaze.

Provençal Sauce

Fry some coarsely chopped tomatoes in smoking oil. Then add salt, pepper, a pinch of sugar, a little chopped parsley and a small piece of garlic. Cook for twenty minutes, having added some chopped mushrooms tossed in oil. Strain and finish with tomato sauce.

Ravigote Sauce

Boil a quarter of a pint of white wine with half that amount of vinegar till it is reduced by half. Add a pint of *velouté*, boil for a few minutes and add finally some pressed shallots pounded with butter.

and a sprinkling of chopped chervil, tarragon and chives.

A cold Ravigote Sauce is made by mixing the following well together:—oil, vinegar, salt, pepper, and chopped onions, capers, parsley, chervil and tarragon.

Red Sauce

A curious sauce, well worth trying, which is used in Spain for cooking fish, is made by pounding together a little garlic and a couple of parboiled, skinned and 'de-pipped' pimentoes. Add a large cupful of water, and mix. This mixture must be added, with a little salt and a drop or two of vinegar, to a cupful of oil which you have brought to the boil in a saucepan. After you have cooked the fish in this, let the sauce reduce, and strain it.

Robert Sauce

Fry in butter a large minced onion without browning it. Add a third of a pint of white wine, reduce this by a third, then add a pint of half-glaze, and simmer for twenty minutes. At the last add a tablespoonful of meat glaze, a pinch of sugar and a teaspoonful of mustard. Do not let it boil again. (You can get a Robert Sauce in the Escoffier products, which only requires the addition of some brown stock to make an excellent hot sauce.)

Saffron Sauce

Saffron is little used generally in this country outside Cornwall, where the baker's windowful of yellow saffron buns is always a mysterious sight to the stranger. However, if any of us have carried away a taste for saffron, this simple sauce may sometimes be used. Simply add to a Béchamel Sauce a pinch of saffron to your taste, and cook it for twenty minutes or so.

Soubise Sauce

This is a more distinguished relative of our homely onion sauce. Fry some minced onions with-

out colouring them, and add some Béchamel Sauce
Cook for half an hour, and season to taste.

This sauce can be made even more distinguished
by the addition of tomato purée or paprika.

Vinaigrette
Sauce

This sauce, which is so pleasant with cold asparagus, is the same as cold Ravigote Sauce, for which
see above.

Vin Blanc
Sauce

This is a simple, but somewhat unorthodox way
of making a White Wine Sauce. Simply make a
brown *roux*, add a glassful of white wine and boil
for a few minutes. Many cooks will hardly agree
with this, but it is quite a good substitute for the
real thing, which is rather complicated to make
Sole *au vin blanc* should be attempted by all.

There are one or two variations of Mayonnaise
Sauce, which I should like to mention.

Andalusian
Sauce

Finish a Mayonnaise Sauce with a purée of
tomatoes, and add to it small dice of red pimentoes.

Bohemian
Sauce

This is a kind of mayonnaise made by mixing
some cold Béchamel Sauce, which has been made
with the addition of the yolks of eggs, with salt,
pepper and vinegar. Add oil in the same way as
for Mayonnaise Sauce, and thin it with tarragon
vinegar.

Chantilly
Sauce

This is an ordinary Mayonnaise Sauce which has
been thinned down with lemon juice instead of
vinegar. Just before serving, some whipped cream
should be folded into it.

Italian
Sauce

A Mayonnaise Sauce made with lemon juice, to
which chopped cooked brains and parsley have been
added.

SAUCES

A purée of apples cooked in white wine mixed with Mayonnaise Sauce and some grated horseradish.

Swedish Sauce

Grated horseradish can be added to a plain mayonnaise with very happy results.

Au Raifort

This is a Mayonnaise Sauce flavoured with mustard. Chopped capers, parsley, gherkins, chervil and tarragon should be added to it, and finally a drop or two of anchovy essence.

Remoulade Sauce

It is sometimes more decorative to have another colour than yellow for one's mayonnaise. It can be turned red by a little pounded flesh of red pimentoes, if it is wanted for meat; or if for fish, then the pounded coral of a hen lobster will do equally well.

Red Mayonnaise Sauce

The simplest way of turning it green is to boil a little spinach, parsley, watercress and chervil for six or seven minutes, squeeze to a pulp, and use the liquid as your colouring agent.

Green Mayonnaise Sauce

Tartare Sauce is a Mayonnaise Sauce strongly seasoned and with chopped onions and chives added to it. Another version adds mustard and parsley, gherkins, capers and tarragon chopped together.

Tartare Sauce

And lastly, there are one or two butters. Black Butter (*Beurre noir*) has been described on page 178. Brown Butter (*Beurre noisette*) is the same, only it is not browned so much.

Brown Butter (Beurre noisette)

White Butter (*Beurre blanc*) is made by putting two finely chopped shallots into a saucepan and adding salt, freshly ground pepper, and a couple of tablespoonfuls of vinegar. Cook a little and then put in, one by one, five pieces of butter the size of

White Butter (Beurre blanc)

a large nut. Stir with a wooden spoon for a few minutes, but see that it does not boil.

Finally, there are the butters for garnishing, or finishing sauces. I will give one or two of the more common ones.

Shrimp Butter   Mix pounded shrimps with their own weight in butter. Strain well and cool.

Lobster Butter   Mix the spawn and creamy parts of a lobster, well pounded together, with their weight in butter, and proceed as before.

Maître d'hôtel Butter   Soften your butter and add to it, for each half-pound, a tablespoonful of chopped parsley, salt, pepper and a few drops of lemon juice.

Other butters, which can be used in garnishing *hors d'œuvres* or for filling hard-boiled eggs, can be made by pounding with good butter such ingredients as Caviare, Curry Powder, Fillets of Red Herrings, Horseradish, Smoked Salmon, Paprika, Pimento, Game, Tunny Fish, and so on. These 'butters' can be enriched with cream.

A LIST OF DISHES FOR WHICH THE RECIPES ARE GIVEN IN *MORE GOOD FOOD*, THE COMPANION VOLUME TO THIS

This list is given in case any reader has failed to find in *Good Food* some favourite recipe for which he was looking. It may be in *More Good Food*.

HORS D'ŒUVRES

Anchoiade Languedocienne; Anchovies; Anchovies and Pimentos; Anchovy *médaillons*; Beans, French; Beetroot *à la crème*; Cabbage, Red; Calf's Brains *à la Robert*; Cauliflower Salad; Caviare; Celeriac; Celery *Bonne Femme*; Cucumber; Cucumber, salted; Cucumbers, stuffed; Eggs; *Foie Gras*; Ham; Ham Cornets; Herrings; Herrings *à la russe*; Herrings, Lucas; Leeks *à la Grecque*; *Macédoine*; Melon; Melon Cocktail; Mullet, Red, *à l'orientale*; Mushrooms; Mussels; Olives; Onions; Oysters; Pimentos *à l'algérienne*; Potato Salad; Prawns; Radishes, simple and prepared; *Salade Russe*; Sardines; Sausages; Shrimps, Potted; Sprats, Smoked; Tomatoes; Tomatoes *à la Monégasque*; Tripe; Tunny Fish; Tunny Fish *Mariette*; Mustard Sauce with Cream.

SOUPS

Almond; Apple; Asparagus; Bean, French; Brussels Sprouts and Carrot; Celeriac; Cherry; Chicken's Liver; Cod's Head; *Consommé à l'estragon*; *Consommé Diablotins*; *Consommé Madrilène*; *Crème Gounod*; Economical; Fish; Hunter's; Lettuce; Pea Pod, Green; Pea, Split; Peas, Dried, and Chervil; Pineapple; Pork and Vegetable; Quick Potato; *Rizzo Figatini*; *Soupe Beaucaire*; *Soupe Flamande*; *Soupe Savoyarde*; Tomato; Watercress.

EGGS

Baked with Anchovies; Baked with Cheese; *Cendrillon*; Cold, *en Surprise*; Cold, with Sweet Corn; Curried; *En cocotte à la Forestière*; *En cocotte à la Reine*; *En cocotte à la Soubise*; Fried, *à l'Américaine*; Fried *à la Fermière*, Fried with Anchovy; Hard-boiled, *à la Bretonne*; In Tartlets; Norwegian; Omelettes *à l'Américaine*; *à la Lyonnaise*; *Bonne Femme*; *Boulonnaise*; *Bretonne*; *Florentine*; *Grand' Mère*; Potato; Sorrel; Tunny Fish; Eggs Poached, in Aspic; Poached, Round; Poached with Cheese and Mushrooms; Rissoles; Scrambled, various; Scrambled, *Châtillon*; *Sur le plat Diable*; *Sur le plat Lilloise*; *Sur le plat Monégasque*; *Sur le plat Omer Pasha*.

FISH

Australian Fish Cakes; *Brill aux Courgettes*.

Cod *à la Boulangère*; and Oyster Pie; Steaks; with Cheese and Potatoes; Salt, *à la Lyonnaise*; Salt, fried; Salt, Ragout.

Crab *aux œufs*; Crawfish (*Langouste*) *à la crème*; Eels *à la Tartare*.

Fish Balls.

Sauce for Fried Fish.

Halibut Steaks with Welsh Rarebit.

Herrings *à la portière*, boiled; fried; grilled.

John Dory.

Langouste à la crème.

Lobster, Cutlets; *Valençay*.

Mackerel *en papillotes*; filleted, *à la crème*; filleted, *au beurre noir*; filleted, grilled; fillets of, *à la Bordelaise*.

Mussels *à la Catalane*.

Oyster Patties; *soufflés*; Oysters *à la crème*; *en coquille*; fried.

Prawn Batter; Prawns, curried.

Red Mullet, broiled; *Grenobloise*.

Rock Salmon *à l'Américaine*.

Salmon Cutlet, baked; *en casserole*; Grilled tail of; Steaks, dressed; Tart.

Scallops, curried.

Shrimp Rolls.

Skate *à la provençale*; with Cheese.

Smelts, grilled.

Sole *à l'étouffé*; *à la provençale*; Cold; *Parisienne*; *Tsarina*; with Cheese and Mushrooms; with Cheese, Onion and Mushrooms; with Cream Sauce; with Risotto.

Sprats, smoked.

Trout *à la Bretonne*; *Doria*.

Turbot *Aïda*; filleted, various; grilled, with bananas; Steaks, *Dugléré*.

Whitebait.

Whiting with Asparagus.

MEAT

Beef, *Bourguignonne*; Brains; Daube of; Fillet of, *au madère*; Mock Venison; Oxtail, grilled; Ox tongue with cherries; Steak, marinated; Tournedos *Montgolfier*; Tournedos *sauté Chasseur*; Tournedos, various; Tournedos with mixed vegetables; Tournedos with bananas.

Bitoques à la russe.

Brains.

Bread, stuffed.

Cauliflower, stuffed.

Cold Meat, fried.

Corned Beef Hash.

Country *pâté*.

Devonshire Squab Pie.

Hachis à la grand'mère; *en portefeuille*.

Ham Dumplings; Mousse.

Keftédès.

Lamb, *à la Lyonnaise*; Jugged; Roast, *à la Béarnaise*; with Turnips.

Mutton, Leg of, *à la Bretonne*; Mutton, onion and apple pie; Onions stuffed with kidney; Mutton on skewers; Sheep's heart, stuffed.

Pork cutlets *au raifort*; Pickled pork and leeks; Pig's Feet *à la Sainte Ménéhould*; Sausage Rolls; Sausages and Apples.

Potatoes, stuffed.

Sweetbreads, various; *en papillote*; in potatoes; with shrimps.

Tongue with cherries.

Tripe *à la Lyonnaise*; Braised.

Veal—Calf's Head; Liver, baked; Dumplings; fried; Escalopes *à l'hongroise*; Escalopes, various; Kidney *à la Bercy*; Kidney *en casserole*; Rolls; Sandwich, stuffed; with mushrooms; with olives; with sour cream.

POULTRY

Chicken *à la limousine*; and corn; *cassolettes*; *coquilles*; curried; *croquettes*; *fricassée* of; fried; *mazagrans*; *pilaff* of; ragout of; *rissoles*; Roast, with Tarragon; *sauté à la Portugaise*; *sauté* (six ways); with Spinach.

Duck, *à la Bordelaise*; Braised, with olives.

Fowl, ragout of.

RECIPES IN *MORE GOOD FOOD*

Goose Drumsticks.
Guinea Fowl *à la Normande*.
Tomato Tart (Chickens' Livers).
Turkey *à la Toscane*; Drumsticks; Stuffing.

GAME

Grouse, Potted.
Hare, *terrine* of.
Leveret *à la provençale*.
Partridge, boiled; with lentils.
Pheasant (Brillat-Savarin's way).
Quails *aux raisins*.
Rabbit *à la poulette*; Flemish; *gibelotte* of; Roast; *sauté, à la minute*;
Venison cutlets; noisettes of.
Woodcock, grilled.

VEGETABLES

Artichoke-Bottom Tart; Artichoke Mould; *purée*.
Asparagus *à la normande*.
Beans, Broad, *à la Bretonne*; *au lard*.
Beans, French, *à l'allemande*; *à la tourangelle*.
Beans, Haricot, *à la Lyonnaise*.
Beans, Runner.
Beetroot, fried.
Brussels Sprouts, *à la crème*; *à la polonaise*; and potato *purée*.
Cabbage, Red, *à la limousine*; with cheese.
Carrots and green peas.
Cauliflower and potato *croquettes*; Cauliflower, stuffed.
Chestnuts, stewed.
Courgettes au beurre; *niçoise*.
Curry, Mixed Vegetable.
Jardinière.
Lettuce, Braised.
Marrow, stuffed.
Mushrooms *au gratin*.
Onion Fritters, Ragout of Onions.
Peas, Green, and Carrots.
Potato Cake, fried; *croquettes*.
Potatoes *à la bretonne*; *à l'irlandaise*; *à la limousine*; *à la normande*; Alsatian;
baked (American fashion); *blésois*; *boulangère*; curried; fried; boiled; grilled;
mashed, with herbs; mashed, *provençale*; mashed, with onions; New, *au
citron*; New, *à la poulette*; with bread sauce; with tomato sauce.
Salsify *à la polonaise*.
Seakale *à la polonaise*.
Sham Whitebait.
Spinach, curried; Subrics.
Tomatoes *Antibes*; *au gratin*; curried; grilled.
Turnips, baked.
Watercress, hot.

SWEETS

Apple Charlotte; Apple, Orange and Lemon Tart.
Apples *à la moscovite*; *Mariette*; stewed; with chocolate.
Apricots *à la colbert*.
Banana Mould.

Bavarois.
Black Currant Leaf Ice.
Brioches, stuffed.
Caramel Junket.
Cherry Tart.
Chestnuts and Prunes.
Confectioner's Cream.
Convent Pancakes.
Cream of Rice.
Crème frite.
Florentine Cream.
Grape-Fruit Cream.
Guava Fool.
Ile flottante.
Lime and Treacle Tart.
Melon *en surprise*; with pineapple.
Méringues aux poires; *Méringues, Pistachio.*
Mock Poached Eggs.
Mont Blanc.
Pain perdu.
Peach Fritters.
Pears, Caramel of; Mary Garden.
Pineapple; hot.
Pistachio Tartlets.
Rhubarb Tart.
Rice Croquettes; Fritters.
Snowballs.
Soufflés, various.
Strawberries *à la créole*; *Romanoff.*
Tangerine Tart.
Three-tiered Cream.

SAVOURY DISHES

Allumettes; Anchovy Biscuits; Anchovy Cheese; *Barquettes Mephisto*;
Bombay Toast; Camembert, Fried; Camembert in Aspic; *Canapé Fédora*;
Canapé Ivanhoe; *Canapé Quo Vadis*; *Canapé Ritchie*; Cheese Fried; Potted;
Savoury; Straws; Tartlets; Wafers; with herbs; *Croûte Diane*; *Croûte Lucullus*;
Croque-monsieur; *Gruyère soufflé*; Ham and Cheese Mould; Herrings' Roes
with Cheese; Macaroni; Mushroom and Bacon Savoury; Mushrooms,
grilled, *à la bourguignonne*; Pilaff Rice; Rice Savoury; Sardine Cigarettes;
Sardine Pancakes; Sardines *au fromage*; Spinach Flan; Spring Onions on
Toast; Tomato Flan; Tomatoes, devilled.

SALADS

Augustin; *Bagatelle*; *Brésilien*; *Canaille*; *Cressonière*; *Dalila*; *Eve*; *Florida*;
Hongroise; *Mariette*; *Midinette*; *Mimosa*; *Poitévine*; *Polonaise*; *Rhénane*;
Tanagra; *Vigneronne.*

SAUCES

Aioli (beurre provençale); *Bigarrade*; *Bretonne*; *Chantilly*; Fennel; *Fines herbes*;
Gloucester; *Gribiche*; *Mayonnaise à la russe*; Mustard Sauce with Cream;
Normande; *Paloise*; Vincent.

FRUIT JELLIES FOR MEAT

Cranberry; Mint; Rowan.

INDEX

INDEX

INDEX

273

INDEX

INDEX

INDEX

INDEX

INDEX

INDEX

INDEX